What people are saying about

An Imaginoscope for Organizers

While imagination is one of the most important topics in organization theory and design, it is unfortur ⅼy one of the least studied. This book by Monika Kostera   ap by allowing readers to rediscover their im॰   s through a series of experiments, starti॰   anging the perspective of observe   ⅼal life, she invites them to parti   ⅼc transmutation of the world of work.

Professor Ghislain Desᵢ   ᵣ Business School

Every once and a while someone from organizational studies writes something that extends far beyond the boundaries and limits of the field, whereby they achieve negentropy. That is, ideas and writing that give us energy and hope. This is what Monika Kostera has achieved here; it is a book of pedagogical ideas, a response to teaching during the Covid pandemic, an exploration of ethnographic phenomenology and a political statement. Not only is the text poetically powerful; it is rich in 'imaginiscope' suggestions, possibilities and interactions, creating a liminal space that we the readers will be eager to enter into and engage with.

Professor Hugo Letiche, Institut Mines-TBS Evry/Paris; The Magic of Organization (edited with J-L Moriceau)

Also by the Author
After the Apocalypse, Zero Books, ISBN: 978-1-78904-480-5

An Imaginoscope for Organizers

Liminal Stories for Liminal Times

An Imaginoscope for Organizers

Liminal Stories for Liminal Times

Monika Kostera

Winchester, UK
Washington, USA

JOHN HUNT PUBLISHING

First published by Zero Books, 2022
Zero Books is an imprint of John Hunt Publishing Ltd., No. 3 East St., Alresford,
Hampshire SO24 9EE, UK
office@jhpbooks.com
www.johnhuntpublishing.com
www.zero-books.net

For distributor details and how to order please visit the 'Ordering' section on our website.

ISBN: 978 1 78904 971 8
978 1 78904 972 5 (ebook)
Library of Congress Control Number: 2021937262

A CIP catalogue record for this book is available from the British Library.

Design: Stuart Davies

UK: Printed and bound by CPI Group (UK) Ltd, Croydon, CR0 4YY
Printed in North America by CPI GPS partners

We operate a distinctive and ethical publishing philosophy in
all areas of our business, from our global network of authors to
production and worldwide distribution.

Contents

To Ilaria Boncori, who inspired me to write this book after having seen a picture I made of Diana's Well in Lectoure. To Beata Nowak, who introduced me to the history of the original 'imaginescope' and told me of the kaleidoscopes that she had made, real and imagined.
And to my students. Thank you, beautiful humans!

Introduction

Just before
just before the wave comes
things lie flat on the ground,
and flutter. some bored,
many restless;
one by one by one,
they do not make up
a whole.
(Monika Kostera, 2021)

Liminal times

Just like the biodiversity of our planet is steadily and alarmingly decreasing – this process has been accelerating in recent years – so is the diversity of the social imaginarium also rapidly diminishing. Philosopher and poet Franco 'Bifo'

Berardi (2019) depicts a social world of imaginative impotence, where preconfigured forms are acquiring a monopolistic status. These forms are technologically and financially driven and forcefully define and limit human creativity. Only the given can be imagined, more of the same: more growth, more pollution, more profits for the billionaires, more inequality...To many of us the outlook does not seem to be very promising. It invites thoughts of extinction, dissipation, collapse.

One hundred years ago, Irish poet William Butler Yeats (1921) wrote the following famous line: 'Things fall apart; the centre cannot hold'. His poem *The Second Coming* portrays a world where sheer chaos is released upon human kind. 'The ceremony of innocence is drowned' the poem proclaims; the worst of us are full of 'passionate intensity' and the best 'lack all conviction'. A similar if less poetic image appears in the writings of contemporary thinkers, invoking philosopher and political theorist Antonio Gramsci's (1971) metaphor of the interregnum, a time when

> [t]he old is dying and the new cannot be born. In this interregnum a great variety of morbid symptoms can appear (p. 556).

Sociologist Zygmunt Bauman (2012), philosopher Edgar Morin (2020) and economist Wolfgang Streeck (2017) all believe we currently live in a time of profound interregnum. Big social structures are dissipating and the socio-economic system that embraces all the important institutions and organizations is dysfunctional. Yet there is no new working system on the horizon. The sanitary, ecological and economic crises are accompanied by a major crisis of imagination. It feels bleak and it looks bleak – and no good news seems to be in sight or, indeed, possible. It is simultaneously a time of conflicting and loud ideas, of sharp polarizations and a kind of feeling of emptiness, a void containing no hope of resolution. In the past there always were more or less utopian visions at hand in times of crisis: of heavenly Jerusalem, of a new golden age, of a perfectly peaceful communism. Nowadays the choice seems to be between one antiquated set of social structures and another, as obsolete, based on rampant nationalism and xenophobia. The centre does not hold, but it is constantly condensing and concentrating, locking in on itself, while using up the resources that surround it. It consists of distilled power, devouring everything in its surroundings. It is like a white dwarf star slowly turning into a black hole. Processes of entropy define the dominant dynamic of systemic death: whoever decides to ride these processes seems to be gaining power and wealth. It seems that only ruthless, irresponsible and nihilistic actions lead to prominence and recognition. Resistance truly seems to be futile. Capitalism is dying and it seems to want to take us all down with it. It has not always been like this.

Western capitalism in the last century, despite undergoing some serious crises, was capable of self-regulation. It was driven by mechanisms of negative feedback, which were used (sooner or later) as a correction of control systems (Obłój and Koźmiński, 1989). It means that feedback signals are used to alter the parameters and modes of how the system works. For example, this is how the thermostat works: when the temperature surpasses certain levels, it triggers an alteration in the heating system causing it to regulate itself to either lower (if it is too hot) or turn up (if it is too cold) the temperature. Applied to big socio-economic systems, it means that negative signals cause an alteration in the way that the system is managed. In times of rampant unemployment new legislation finally appears, protecting employees in relation to the employers. Women demand equal pay for equal work and after times of protest and struggle the system finally incorporates some adjustments in this respect. People unionize and demand more free time and finally the battle has some effects and paid leave is extended for the workforce.

Since the 1980s, neoliberal capitalism has abandoned this mode of social renewal and adopted instead a different control mechanism, based on positive feedback. Now, instead, corrective signals lead to the enhancement of existing processes. Social protests against the worsening of work conditions and a de facto decrease of standard pay in developed countries have led to the moving of production to poor countries where the employees are paid much less, and work conditions are much worse, creating massive unemployment in former industrialized areas. Protests against wars, inequality, racism, seem to be leading nowhere, only attracting more and more open institutionalized violence and persecution. Imagine a broken radiator: when it gets too hot, a broken mechanism gone barking mad turns the heating up even more. That is how neoliberalism works. It produces vicious loops of responses to problems based on the logic of 'more of the same'. We end up in a wildly lopsided world, profoundly out of balance. Economic journalist Grace Blakely (2020) depicts a world where the power of trade unions has been all but crushed, the management of organizations has become almost completely financialized, most powerful institutions are operating outside of democratic control and towards aims that are divorced from categories of the common good. Economist Guy Standing (2019) argues that the common good had been depleted, even robbed, and transformed into a source for further and seemingly endless enrichment of increasingly anonymous investment funds. The system is dead but it is still feeding on the living planet we all inhabit. And yet it is more and more desperately obvious to many of us, humans, that we cannot continue on this path, lest we destroy our civilization and maybe the whole planet too.

And yet there does not seem to be a way out, *there is no alternative,* to use the famous catchphrase of British prime minister Margaret Thatcher. That is another effect of a system controlled by positive feedback loops; it leads constantly and persistently to the enhancement of existing processes. This unifies power and consolidates the system. At the same time, it prevents regeneration, renewal and adaptation to an increasingly complex environment. Power in a complex system should not be uniform, but rather reflect its complexity. The cybernetic law of requisite variety (Ashby, 1958) posits that the complexity of the regulator should match the complexity of the controlled system: the number of states that its control mechanism is capable of attaining (its variety) must be greater than or equal to the number of states in the system being controlled if the system is to keep stable. Applied to social systems such as organizations and institutions, it means that management needs to be at least as complex and diverse as the organization managed. Not just to keep an equilibrium but to be able to develop. Systems learn by negative feedback and with the number of feedback loops the learning gets increasingly profound; from the simple corrections of the thermostat, via looking for causes (double loop learning) to learning how to learn (triple loop). But with positive (instead of negative) feedback as the main regulatory mechanism, the system ceases to learn. It also loses its memory. Neoliberalism is capitalism that has lost its memory: it is a system suffering from dementia. It is unable to learn and lacks imagination. This – at a time when we need alternatives more than ever to leave the void of the interregnum collectively and construct a new system that would be more humane and ecologically sound than the former one. It is a liminal situation and a liminal time, and it calls for extra power of imagination.

Anthropologist Victor Turner (1970) described the liminal as the middle stage in rites of passage, betwixt and between ordinary social interactions, when people play social roles according to their rank, profession, age, status and so on. When people progress between roles, cultures provide them with rites of passage. They transport a person from one role to another with an indeterminate phase in between. This transitional moment is called the liminal phase. During this period people experience uncertainty and have little control over what is happening and even less sense of stability. However, it is a moment of great potential; hierarchies can be altered, even reversed, continuity of the traditional system may become questioned, and new scenarios for communication developed. These powerful moments can bring about change and renewal not just for the person concerned but for the whole society. But they can also unleash destruction, anxiety and disquiet. They are essential for re-birth and regeneration but difficult to make sense of using the categories and narratives of the old role, or old structures of meaning.

The interregnum is a kind of collective super-liminal period. Most books and articles depicting the interregnum of our times and pondering how to get out of the toxic limbo, speak of the necessity of crossing a systemic void, getting from the deterministic course towards destruction to a future system which would make it possible to preserve life and give humans a hope. This book addresses the void itself, seen as a liminal space/time, betwixt between working and more stable systems with defined social roles, problem solutions and language for communication in and about organizations. This book proposes to use this time by turning to imagination and reverie – a natural and fruitful response to such times as we now inhabit, as philosopher Gilles Hieronimus (2020) advises. For this a special capability is crucial.

Negative capability

Romantic poet John Keats speaks of the

> Negative Capability, that is when a man is capable of being in uncertainties, Mysteries, doubts, without any irritable

reaching after fact & reason – Coleridge, for instance, would let go by a fine isolated verisimilitude caught from the Penetralium of mystery, from being incapable of remaining content with half knowledge (Keats, 1958, pp. 193–4).

Negative here does not mean something bad, wrong or lacking – it is a way of embracing mystery. There exists a form of theology, apophatic theology, also known as *via negativa*, which is a quest for God by negation, by pointing out what cannot be said or defined about the godhead. What is beyond perception can, according to this way of thinking, only be grasped by not grasping. In a similar vein, the 'negative' in negative capability implies an ability to refrain from defining and categorizing, not necessarily by proclaiming what *it is not* but by desisting to name everything we see. Keats advises to practise it not so much for theological purposes (and he rejected conventional Christianity) but as a way of being in the world. He viewed negative capability as a way of confronting what we cannot understand, through abstaining from the nascent urge to explain. Aimed at the human subject as much as at the surrounding world, it represents a kind of doubt about the relationship between who we are and what we see. To have negative capability is to know how to prolong attention, to refrain from rationalizations or conclusions when we encounter that which defies comprehension. This approach encompasses both modesty and bravery. Modesty, because we thus admit that we do not understand something. Bravery, because it is human to name and tame, even before we take a good look at something. But there is more to it than that. Keats considers negative capability to be a way of gaining new insight – by way of refusing to immediately recognize and know. There is an ocean of truth all around us – to borrow the beautiful metaphor of American novelist Ursula Le Guin (1995) in *Four Ways to Forgiveness*. We cast out a net onto it and bring back only a fragment, a particle, a flash of what is infinite, inexhaustible, unknowable. Human knowledge is fragmentary, local, essentially arbitrary – which does not mean irrelevant, or unimportant. On the contrary, every grain of truth is a reflection of something immense. If we dare to question our own assumptions, this grain may be able to teach us something new.

To Keats, this does not mean the adoption of an inquisitive distance, as it does not have to mean to us, in today's turbulent world. A sense of mystery is not a disinterested pursuit for its own sake, or for knowledge as such, it is a quest for something greater than ourselves: 'with a great poet the sense of Beauty overcomes every other consideration, or rather obliterates all consideration' (Keats, 1958). A poet is ready to give up 'reaching after fact & reason' (ibid.) to strive for the *intensity* of presence that is art.

Negative capability is important not just to poets but to all of us, including organizers. Organization theorist Robert French (2001) upholds the value it has for organizational change. Change is threatening and the typical organizational reactions to it are, on the one hand, 'management of change', or impositions of rules that aim at forcing the organization into a scenario of development that leaves little or no space for fluctuation and adaptation. On the other hand, employees fear that every change will be for the worse, and with considerable reason. As one of my students put it some time ago: even single change introduced in recent years has been for the worse. Small wonder people resist such change, if they can, or numbly go along with it, seeing 'no alternative' and losing heart. Instead of this French reminds organizers of Keats' negative capability, which would signify a completely new managerial approach to change: to live with it and tolerate ambiguity and paradox. Negative capability embraces the poetic imagination instead of ideologies of control based on what French, after Needleman, regards as dispersal of energy by strategies implying rushing into action, breaking down problems into manageable bits. Negative capability would help organizational participants to learn and have one's mind changed. It involves the development of mature intuition of all participants.

Leadership also stands to gain much from negative capability, as it encourages leaders to be open to the world and to others, accepting that one cannot know or understand everything (Simpson, French and Harvey, 2002). The 'reflexive inaction' of the leader means the ability to wait, refrain from fast decisions, to listen and to observe. It is the opposite of the current culture of rapid reaction and performativity, so it is unlikely to gain many followers in the present mainstream of management education. But it is definitely a useful alternative. French philosopher Ghislain Deslandes (2020) calls this alternative 'weak management'. It is an approach to management based on a human conception of control, recognition of fallibility, attention to weak signals. Nowadays it forms a radical alternative but it is rooted in ancient wisdom: by renouncing aspirations to omnipotence a leader becomes truly capable and able to face responsibility.

These are important issues. But negative capability is not just something for managers and leaders. In today's profoundly uncertain times it can help human beings to simply stay sane. Humans crave sense as much as we crave water and bread. With negative capability we can experience doubt and hold on to it, without immediately having to resort into one of the existing categories: conservative, liberal, national, foreign. Instead of fighting wars for an excluding nation or a fixed identity, we can remain, for a time, open to the world even in the state of current disarray. This state of mind can help us to doubt and examine, search and persist, and not be satisfied or dulled by the seemingly obvious and inevitable. It enables radical questioning not only of commonly held truths but of the assumptions that they are constructed upon. And in order to communicate and make sense of the world despite not hurrying to name it and categorize away, we may need something instead of ready labels that is just as human as the customary definitions. We need imaginative stories.

At the 2014 US National Book Awards, Ursula Le Guin expressed a conviction that writers can imagine and tell of a different world than the one we, today, tend to see as the only one possible. 'We live in capitalism,' she said,

> its power seems inescapable,' but then, so did the divine right of kings. Any human power can be resisted and changed by human beings. Resistance and change often begin in art. Very often in our art, the art of words (Le Guin, 2014).

Not just professional writers, but all of us can do that, by freeing the artists and storytellers in ourselves as well: in sociologists, engineers, electricians, politicians and cleaners. Nobody will fight for a better world without seeing it first. Each springtime of the peoples has its stories and poems, music and art. They tend to come first. Only later arrive the theories, ideologies, policies. According to psychologist Jerome Bruner (1991) stories are part and parcel of who we are as human beings and how we communicate and make sense of the world. Humans put experience and wisdom into stories. We tell stories to learn and to teach but also out of a need for sociality, sharing and passing on something that turns into common good when narrated to others. Organization complexity theorist Hugo Letiche (2021) upholds that stories have the distinctive capacity to express layered complexity and adopt a multi-perspective view, while at the same time being vivid, meaningful and direct.

A storytelling collective called Dark Mountain calls for different stories which would be suitable for our times. The old plots of progress and civilization are no longer effective in evoking ideas of change and renewal. Stories have always been part of the human condition and storytellers 'have been treated with respect and, often, certain wariness' (*Uncivilization*, 2014, p. 18). The ancient art of storytelling can help us to access the domain from which change and renewal can be drawn: imagination and mystery – and we need that more than ever in our difficult and bleak times. A large number of authors representing different walks of life echo this call, from sociologists and psychologists, via organization theorists and economists, including also representatives of the so-called STEM sciences occasionally. Biology professor David Sloan Wilson (2021) expressed a strong conviction of the urgent need for stories that would reflect the human condition better than the ego- and individual-centred ones that now dominate in the public discourses. He points out that '[s]tories are powerful because they are vehicles for imbibing moral worldviews', and if the story and its worldview 'resonates with the reader, then the reader gobbles up the story and wishes to make it a reality'. A good story can help to change the world. It helps to

> expand public discourse beyond narrow reforms so as to honestly engage with and tackle the environmental, ethical, and spiritual crisis facing our world and envision and develop strategies to achieve a loving and just world in which people overcome utilitarian consciousness, treat one another as embodiments of the sacred, and respond to the universe with awe, wonder, and radical amazement (Tikkun, 2020).

Without Moses, the Red Sea will not open. Not just because he was a great prophet, but because he had a calling to hear and see far away through the waves. And he knew how to tell the others about it.

But can we? How would this be possible in a tremendous crisis of imagination? How can we imagine when the imaginarium is so impoverished that, as psychologist James Hillman (2017) put in, part of the human space – the inner space where creation takes place, is dead? There are no gods, no Muses, no poetry. For this vital task this book proposes a simple yet sophisticated instrument that enables one to see, hear and feel the imagination – the imaginoscope.

The imaginoscope

The imaginoscope is a device used to observe and experience objects and events taking place in the imagination. It is made entirely of imaginary matter.

It was first invented (as 'imaginescope') in the 1970s by the Polish sociologist and writer Stanisław Moskal, who wrote about this piece of equipment under the pseudonym Śledź Otrembus Podgrobelski. He published a book titled *The Introduction to Imaginescopy* (republished 2009), written in the style of science fiction, about a new scientific discipline, 'imaginescopy', focused on the exact studies of the imagination. The ultimate aim of the discipline was to extend the domain of the imagination by the application of scientific methods and measurements. The imaginescope could be constructed of wood, utilizing its natural characteristics, and in particular any gnarls and holes that can be used as 'sight vane' trough through which the researcher can behold the imaginary object of study. But it could also be found in nature or architecture, as a particular kind of tube or crack that opens out into something quite different from the ordinary surroundings (Image 2 represents my take on a spontaneously encountered imaginoscope). The inventor explains that the matter surrounding the lens seems to create a kind of amplifying field that affects the waves of consciousness that flow from the observing eye and into the world. It produces an empathic connection between the outside and inside spaces. By looking through the imaginescope the observer sees reality extended by the imagination and can train herself to later see it the same way even without the device.

The book attracted a fandom, including more conventional sci-fi readers, as well as (non-imaginary) social scientists. For example, literary scholar Przemysław Kaliszuk (2017) claims that the imaginescope helps to map liminal areas between *real science* and *(science) fiction*. By virtue of being a pretext to spin liminal stories, it connects embodied desires to aspirations of the imagination. It also makes the imagination an object of study of a scientific discipline that is neither psychology, nor psychiatry. Imagination is presented as something real, not a product of the mind. Imaginescopy also differs from philosophy and especially from phenomenology – imagination is not a phenomenon. It is a reality that is connected to intentionality and human will which, in Podgrobelski's writings, always hover close to sexuality, but it remains unclear whether and how the two are connected. In the end, it does not really matter because it turns out that science and art are so closely entangled in the imaginesope that they provoke and yield complex amalgamates of insights and sensations. At the heart of the stories of the imaginescope lies a surrealist proposition: to extend reality with the help of the imagination. Thinking, observing, writing are no longer subordinated to scientistic procedures and ideals. But neither are they divorced from reason. It seems that the key to the successful achievement of all this, of the establishing of a liminal scientific and artistic project, is to be found in language. Kaliszuk believes that talking and writing creates a space where all this becomes possible. The stories about the imaginescope do not rely on certainty – rather, they question, doubt and admit ambivalence – without resorting to ridicule or sarcastic nihilism.

Even though the emphasis on stories is as central in this book as in Moskal's original, the imaginoscope calls for different stories than did the imaginescope. The imaginoscope of this book is a multisensory practice and a quest. Its image (fig. 2) comes from a lovely old French town, Lectoure, in the region of Occitanie, where I came across an element of an old water fountain called Diana's Well that reminded me of a kaleidoscope, and I photographed it. A colleague and friend, organization theorist Ilaria Boncori, suggested that I write a book about it. Even though strongly reminiscent of it, this instrument is not an imaginescope (a device to clearly see and measure the imaginary) but rather an imaginoscope (a tool to see and experience the imaginary). The original imaginescope had, furthermore, a phallic imagery (Kaliszuk, 2017), whereas the predominance of the element of water and the presence of the goddess Diana signals the boldly feminine character of the imaginoscope.

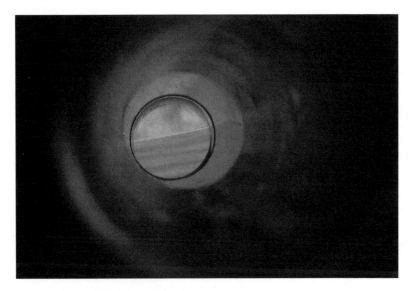

The imaginoscope is, then, not just a viewing device. It can be applied to the eye, to the ear, to the heart and even to the soul. It helps to see, to hear and feel patterns where there are none in a fractured reality of our liquid times. These patterns can then be turned into stories using various plots, including some very old ones – the archetypes – very powerful patterns and compelling plots that have been guiding human storytelling for centuries and millennia (more about archetypes in Chapter 3.1.). This book helps to create an imaginoscope out of imaginary matter and to use it on a quest for what is unknown and uncertain. It is relatively stable and can be used for prolonged periods of time to train the mind and the heart by reflection and practical exercises. It can be used individually and collectively to activate and mobilize creative organizing impulses. In other words, this book proposes intellectual, symbolic and poetic insights that, ultimately, can be used by people who wish to *organize differently*. These creative organizing ideas and practices are the final aim of the quest.

Each chapter is a step on the quest and contains a reflective part, offering a collection of ideas and a language that can be used to invent and communicate the reader's own ones; as well as a practical part, consisting of an imaginative exercise and inspiring examples of how it can be used. The book should be read chronologically for best effect. The role of the first chapter is to awaken imaginative consciousness that can be useful for organizers, and the following ones develop it further, until the last one, which proposes an interactive realization of what has been learned throughout the quest. This is a short book but should preferably be read slowly, not as a page turner but, rather, as something of a modern Theoderich's Guide to the Holy Land (1986), which, too, is a collection of knowledge and imagination. The latter is one of the best known and most widely used of the medieval pilgrims' guides to Jerusalem and the Holy Land. Written around 1172 by the German monk Theoderich, it is a complete guide to the city's sacred sites and history, as well as to the legends and places of historical interest in the medieval Crusader State. It is not a straightforward factual guide, but a book that was intended to (and in fact was) used by people who could not travel and so undertook an imaginary pilgrimage.

As is this book. The subsequent chapters move the reader forward, not necessarily on a geographical map – rather, they are a guide in the domain of the imagination. Ideas and insights help to create and calibrate the imaginoscope so that it suits a section of the domain. The reader can experience different things on the way and bring them into the next stage of the journey. The chapters and indeed the whole journey are based on classes I was teaching at the Institute of Culture, The Jagiellonian University in 2020, which was a most unusual time. The spring semester started as usual, in the institute's classes on campus. Then, in the middle of a lecture, came the announcement that the campus was being closed due to the COVID-19 pandemic. We were watching the final scene from a movie I was showing to the students. Then we rather abruptly said goodbye. I was confident we would see each other in a few weeks' time. But a few days later we received correspondence from the then dean for teaching that there would be a lockdown and all teaching was, for an indeterminate period of time, to be conducted online. He wrote that he trusted our professional judgement to do whatever was right under these extreme circumstances, in order to teach students to the best of our abilities. He asked more experienced teachers to offer support and guidance to the less experienced ones, if they asked for such help. He expressed his respect for and sympathy with the whole teaching community. A similar letter arrived later from the director of the institute and so the greatest teaching experiment of my academic career began. Many of the students moved away from campus during lockdown, back to their family homes which were often located in the countryside, without reliable internet access. Besides, none of us was really interested in pretending that everything was normal – I received much personal communication from my students where they spoke of their distress, feelings of uncertainty and loneliness – but also a kind of indefinite hope and openness, a very fragile yet extremely important state of mind. I promised them that we would use the time wisely and empathically, to explore the fundamental and unknown, as well as to learn about what we do and should know. We did not have regular online classes following the ordinary time schedule, but met on zoom from time to time, in large groups or individually. Presence was not required on the part of the students. I used to send them teaching material via email every week: brief summaries of the current class as well as recommended literature and films to watch. Every week I also sent them a personal assignment, such as the ones narrated in this book. I asked them for short individual answers by email. This worked well and after the semester was over, the students expressed their satisfaction and joy concerning this mode of teaching and learning. However, the old dean for teaching was replaced by a new one in the new semester and the experiment was abandoned: both teachers and students are now, as of my writing these words, required to follow a pre-set schedule and participate in synchronous classes on an internet platform. Nonetheless, we who had been teaching during that highly unusual semester learned a lot – as did the students, to judge both from private communication and from their formal evaluations. I am convinced that what we all learned was not just the more or less standard course content, but something that school, or university (especially in liquid modernity), does not teach.

One can say these were classes in negative ability.

1. Departure: Looking and seeing

1.1. How to look? What to see?

When travelling by other means than your own two feet or private transport, you usually need a ticket confirming you are entitled to go on board. For the journey in the imagination the required ticket attests the attention of the passenger. This chapter provides a way to acquire the attention necessary for the journey: by looking and seeing.

The famous two introductory sentences to John Berger's beautiful and highly influential book *Ways of Seeing* (1972) state:

> Seeing comes before words. The child looks and recognizes before it can speak. (p. 7).

Seeing is more than just taking in something by the sense of sight, Berger explains – it establishes our place in the world.

We see and are aware that we can be seen. John Berger was a British art critic but also a poet and painter: when he spoke of seeing, he meant much more than just perceiving. Seeing is immersive and it is about being part of something much bigger than oneself. When it comes to representations of vision, such as art, this aspect of seeing become even more evident: they carry meaning. Images are not just things 'out there': they are bestowed with a capacity to 'conjure up the appearances of something that was absent' (p. 10). Looking at images – and, indeed, creating images, brings the observer into a conversation with the observed and with other observers. This is also an important lesson taught to the traveller in the Imagination by ethnography.

The ethnographic method called non-participant observation (see more about it in e.g. Harding and Kostera, 2021) is all about active looking in order to see things that elude ordinary, everyday view. The ethnographer strives at remaining an outsider in social situations in the observed field and not only refrains from taking part in them but approaches them as if seen for the first time in his or her life. This was the method of choice of authors such as philosophers Michel de Certeau (1988) and Walter Benjamin (1999), who both used to walk around in cities and tried to grasp their elusive aura. This method is based on a conscious effort to focus on the immediate moment as intensely as possible. A way of seeing is adopted similar to what Berger speaks about when he says that 'seeing comes before words'. Things are seen afresh, without their names, and then, narrated anew, not necessarily in the same way as usually and not necessarily with the use of the everyday categories. In fact, the point of ethnography is to find new categories and configurations of the everyday, in order to understand it better. The researcher is like a traveller betwixt and between known worlds, attentive and curious about everything, refraining from categorizations judgement, a light of pure consciousness immersed in the surroundings yet not quite there at all, devoid of a normal role and thus almost socially invisible. If, as organization researcher Barbara Czarniawska upholds, culture is *the medium of life* (1991), then observing it takes for humans what it would take for a fish to observe water: unlikely. We take it for granted, because we grow up in it; because it forms the lens through which we see and understand the world. Culture offers categories of meaning and human is a meaning-making animal. We assign meaning to the surrounding world in order to create an order that we call civilization. When we grow up we learn that things have names and that they are related to each other, that they form larger groups of related things and that we have a position vis a vis these groups. A ball is a toy but it also belongs in the category of sport accessories. There are different kinds of balls: a football and a volleyball are similar but they are used differently. The human player is supposed to do certain things with a football and others with a volleyball – and there are rules that make a game possible when several human beings are present and ready to be at the ball. Social scientist Karl Weick (1995) argues that humans rely on sensemaking because it is something that gives

> plausibility and coherence, something that is reasonable and memorable, something that embodies past experience and expectations, something which resonates with other people, something that can be constructed retrospectively but also can be used prospectively, something that captures both feeling and thought, something that allows for embellishment to fit current oddities, something that is fun to contrast. In short, what is necessary in sensemaking is a good story. (pp. 60-61)

That is why stories are not just a pleasure and a pastime that human beings have been engaging in since time immemorial, but play a much more fundamental role in our life; they are part of who we are, of the human condition. Weick speaks of two main elements of sensemaking which he refers to as frame and cue. The frame is something large, a kind of shared vocabulary of taken-for-granted ideas of the social, of the surroundings, norms and traditions. Thanks to the frame the experiences of others before us are ready for us to use: the frame consists of knowledge turned symbolic which can be transmitted across generations. Sensemaking happens by connecting present cues derived from an actual situation to existing frames and stories serve as a connecting device. Every situation has many possible meanings which can crystallize by interpretation. Let's say I am in a modern urban setting and there are several people around me with fruits and vegetables placed in front of them in boxes. What is happening here? There are cues in the situation we react to, such as: urban, people, produce, boxes. We use the frames that are available to us. Is it a marketplace? A gardeners' fair? Or an artwork? We place the situation within some context: people stop to buy fruit and veg but they all pay in cash and receive no receipts, and there are no stalls. A marketplace, then, but not an official one. The story we tell ourselves to understand the situation includes protagonists: the farmers selling produce and the buyers stopping to buy. There is a plot that transcends the situation and which is mainly implied: the authorities have closed down the big farmers' market in the city centre but there are still people who want to buy and sell fresh veg. So this makeshift marketplace appears here, not quite where the old market used to be, but visible to passers-by. And not too close to the police station.

But is it really a marketplace? In order to see it as something entirely different, such as a work of art, demands a different frame, derived from the world of the arts. The arts educated passer-by perceived not only the sellers – and buyers – but also other subtle cues. Here is a strategically placed mirror and a photographer ready to take an 'unselfie' of you amid apples and pears. And here is an honesty box with bizarre graphics. Yes, people are selling and buying but isn't it a bit more ceremonial, special, like the *Why Do You Shop?* project founded by Judith Wilske in the 1990s (Venkatesh, 1999)? It was a real business company, and at the same time, an art performance. A group of artists and researchers wanted to find the existential reasons for shopping so they set up a mobile stall located in a stylish caravan in which they undertook several road trips in Europe. They were selling designer goods and gadgets, and asking buyers questions about their reasons for and ideas of shopping. Basically, they wanted to know:

> There are so many questions you can ask of daily life, why do you read a book? why do you watch TV? Why do you listen to music? And so on. Where does, in this list of questions, Why Do You Shop? fit and what is its special significance? Is it because you are an economist and you want to understand how the economy functions? Or is there something about shopping that strikes you as being special? In other words, I do a lot of things every day and I don't in fact shop every day? Where does this come from? (Wilske in Venkatesh, 1999, p. 299)

They staged a shopping ceremony, which involved real selling and buying, as well as chatting and interviewing,

> a typical situation is that we just stand in the middle of a shopping area with our wonderful mobile shopping caravan, which is an old American SV, by the way. From the outside you can see our logo which is Why Do You Shop? so our whole caravan is very specially designed as a stage. And if I say as a stage, I mean that we designed it in a way that people get curious to find out what's going on inside. (ibid., p. 301)

The project also involved photography and fashion design which were exhibited in the van but also elsewhere, during talks and presentations. There was no predetermined agenda, the project was fairly open towards both its dimensions: as an art performance and as a business. So, in our example, the makeshift fruit and veg stalls can play a similar role. The buyers are real buyers but also the audience. Perhaps a person not used to looking at art would be able to guess what it was if she noticed the dissonant cues and let them question her taken-for-granted 'street market' frame. One does not have to consciously engage with it, just allow some impulse: curiosity, interest, surprise and so on, to become the driving force to question and explore. By the way, this is exactly what the *Why Do You Shop?* project provoked.

But to see the frame itself needs looking at in the ethnographic sense, a bold application of the imaginoscope. If the frame is a lens through which we perceive the world, then we need to turn our conscious gaze towards it – and it is as difficult as studying one's own pair of eyes just by using them to look. To use the words of organization theorist Linda Smircich (1983), the cultural frame structuralizes our perception. We do not see the 'world as such', but as it appears through the frame. First of all, our senses are limited. Secondly, we understand each situation in a context. Everything: fact, method, impression, idea, thing, is always part of a context and may only be taken in by humans in relation to it (Garfinkel, 1976). To be able to look this way it is necessary to focus consciously and see what is usually unseen. When explaining the topic of non-participant ethnographic observation to my students I sometimes use a metaphor, which helps them to grasp what it takes: observation is like looking at a stereogram. When we first see a stereogram, it looks like a normal, but rather boring, postcard. It consists of rows of identical patterns such as, for instance, tiny geometrical figures. But once we are able to look at it in a certain way, and fans of stereograms know a lot of tricks that support the re-focus of sight, a new dimension starts to emerge. A wholly different image appears and it is three dimensional. It has usually not much in common with the pattern which was visible at first glance, even if it uses it as its structure. And it is not boring, it can be regarded from several points of view. Similarly, if we focus on the patterns of human behaviour around us and look beyond it, suddenly a new image emerges. Everyday scenes become interesting and many dimensional and show something which was there all the time but was not visible by the distracted everyday sight. When my students go out and observe for the first time, they often choose popular, generally accessible places, such as shopping centres, railway stations, concert halls, schools, buses, halls on campus. These seemingly well-known places reveal their secrets to them and, as one of my older students put it, provide an opportunity to become a child again. Children are rarely bored when they explore the world. Children, ethnographers and mystics tend to see what is unique and thus interesting; their world is often fascinating, but also uncertain and full of surprises.

Try to imagine inhabitants of a distant planet out there, in space. These creatures are sapient and technologically advanced. But they are different from us Earthlings; they possess none of the main human senses: no sight, hearing, smell, taste *or* touch. But they have seven other senses! Senses that we human beings do not have. And now, imagine them entering the room where you presently are. What do they perceive? Do they perceive you? Do you perceive them? Maybe they *are* here?...

What would one see in the makeshift marketplace if the ethnographic look was adopted? Maybe something like this:

The space is densely crowded, packed with people, mingling around small tabletops of the kind used by campers. On each table there is a cardboard box full of vegetables and

24

fruits. Each is accompanied by a person, standing or sitting by the table. I approach one of them. The box is full of apples and pears, arranged in two compartments. Another box contains root vegetables, similarly arranged into separate compartments in the box. The place emanates a powerful smell of greens, melting sweetness and fresh earth. The produce comes in various shapes and shades. Not every tabletop carries boxes. On several of them vegetables and fruit cascade more loosely down. People mingle among the stalls, stop to look and chat with each other and with the persons standing or siting by the tables. One woman dressed in a heavy grayish coat takes an apple in her hand and inspects it, lifting it to her face. She then asks the person standing behind the table for the price. Hearing the answer, she nods smilingly and asks for a kilogram of these apples. The other person also smiles and puts several apples into a brown paper bag and places them in one pan of some small scales. In the other she puts some weights, looking like they were made of old brass. The weights are of a dull grayish colour. They exchange a few sentences about the weather. I have an impression of finding myself in the midst of one of Rebecca Campbell's paintings, perhaps Abundance, depicting a vegetable garden with rows of cabbages, carrots, gigantic leeks, and many other kinds of greens, where some small animals eye the crops and each other hungrily, fearfully or maybe just curiously? Or maybe The Pantry, a methodical cornucopia: shelves full of tempting fruit, vegetables, meats, pastry and preserves. Reflecting on these associations, I discover I am staring at a table which is different from the others. Instead of fruits or veg it contains a large shape, presumably a cardboard box with posters pasted on its four sides. They are all old ads for a theatre that used to operate in the 1980s in this exact location. I suddenly have a flash of recollection of how I used to come here now and again to see different performances and my memory slows down to explore a powerfully staged Ionesco in which my consciousness gets momentarily immersed. After a moment I look up and see the new shining high rises encircling the spot where I stand, radiating a distant cold and something of a sanitized aspect, devoid of smell yet as if sticky, putrescent.

An attempt to look through the imaginoscope – ethnographically – first unravelled a number of scenes related to markets and marketplace behaviours. But then the meeting with an element not belonging in the scenery triggered an association with art, which channelled, at first, introspective reflections, and then a sudden sense of connection to the space throughout time.

So, briefly, the imaginoscope helps us to see the frames. Ethnography can teach us how to then look through and beyond them The main lessons are the following:

- Avoid all interpretation and categorization. Just look and focus, as if you saw the situation around you and all its components for the first time in your life. Do not think of what has been or what will be, do not make plans of what to make of it. Try to shut down the running commentary in your mind.
- Do not evaluate or judge. Forget your ideas of good and bad, right or wrong, beautiful and ugly. The feelings of awe, terror, contentment may come at you but you should allow them to come unaccompanied by words. Name them only when you feel the words formed in your head are not part of everyday associations; when they feel like poetry, not labelling.
- Be interested in everything, even the 'boring' things, perhaps particularly in them. Focus on the small details, as if you were an explorer with a mission to record every element of an unknown culture. Try to see the main

sequences of actions, as well as what is going on in the background. Register and take in with all your senses, it takes more than sight to see. Listen, feel, breathe, smell, take in. Now re-focus; let the background become the foreground and vice versa. Some people consciously concentrate on what they usually omit, such as the ceiling in a supermarket, the faces of people in a shop, the light on the walls in a church.

- Remain an outsider. Do not get used to what you observe. Find more and more things you have not noticed before. See the connections between them.
- Take notes if you can; it is really difficult to keep all this in mind.

It is a conscious attempt to experience the here and now. Usually we are immersed in it but are blind to it, in the words of Michel de Certeau:

> The ordinary practitioners of the city live 'down below,' below the thresholds at which visibility begins. They walk – an elementary form of this experience of the city; they are walkers, Wandersmanner, whose bodies follow the thicks and thins of the urban 'text' they write without being able to read it. These practitioners make use of spaces that cannot be seen; their knowledge of them is as blind as that of lovers in each other's arms. The paths that correspond in this intertwining, unrecognized poems in which each body is an element signed by many others, elude legibility. It is as though the practices organizing a bustling city were characterized by their blindness. (de Certeau, 1988, p. 94)

Observation is about being attentive. The person equipped with the imaginoscope endeavours to perceive reality as directly as possible, without the mediation of cultural meanings. This is of course impossible, humans are creatures immersed in culture and cannot live otherwise, not very long anyway. Culture is the medium of meaning, the lens through which we make sense and give sense. But if we give something the incredible power of our full attention we can, for a moment, take a peek beyond the layers of the culturally known and defined. Symbolic interactionists speak of *epiphanic moments* (Denzin, 2002), glimpses of clarity and staggering insight. The Canadian bard Leonard Cohen describes them in this poem:

My will cut in half
And freedom between
For less than a second
Our lives will collide
The endless suspended
The door open wide (Cohen, 2006, p. 1)

1.2. Practice: Looking

Observe very intensively the space of your home for 15-30 minutes. Focus only on what is here now. During the observation, do not talk to anyone, do not even take notes or photos. If you like, imagine you are a visitor from another planet or from another, distant civilization (e.g. ancient Greece). Discover one thing: an object, a phenomenon, a flow, an impression that you have never seen or focused on before. It can be something small and simple, such as a scratch on the wallpaper, or fundamental and large (I will not give an example so as not to suggest anything to you). After the observation, write it down in your notebook or take a photo.

What did you discover? How did it happen? Why did you not focus on it before? What did it change in your relationship to the familiar space? What follows are some of the responses I got from my students to this question. Reflect on how they correspond with your own discovery. Are there any similarities,

28

any differences between what the others saw and what you yourself perceived? What do they tell you about your space, about yourself?

Natalia looked around but her gaze was attracted by the view outside, so she went out to the terrace:

> During the observation on the terrace of the house, my attention was drawn to the tree on the border of my garden. Until now, I did not pay attention to it – just one of the many trees behind the house. This time, however, it caught my eye. This tree is distinguished by its height – it is much higher than other plants and shrubs around it. The branches are not branchy – the tree shoots upwards rather than to the sides, and they are covered with white, tiny flowers that fall to the ground in stronger gusts of wind. The trunk is relatively thin and straight, with yellow and green lichens in places. (Natalia)

Anna concentrated on the inside of her flat:

> ...although the space of my apartment is not very large, I can certainly say that the whole thing is arranged with attention to detail. Focusing on what is inside, I noticed a small box on the bookshelf – the light was reflecting on it. The box looks like it has a story of its own, and when closed – it seems to hide secrets. The object is located in such a place that its colours change depending on the time of day. (Anna)

Nina also started looking inside her flat, but it was the human inhabitants that attracted her attention:

> Everyone in the house was at home so I could see if there was anything that never caught my attention or if there was any new behaviour by my family (dad, mom and sister).

29

At least that's what I thought, because after 4 minutes my parents decided to go shopping. I did not notice anything new at home. The only new behaviour was that my sister became irritated by my silence. After 10 minutes, my parents came back from their shopping tour, but they did not bring any groceries. Mom decided to plant tomatoes and herbs on the balcony. So she bought land, pots and seeds. This is the first time she creates a mini garden. You could see the contentment and excitement in her face and gestures. (Nina)

Paulina's observation also contained something unusual.

As it turned out, the observation of my tiny room in the attic from a different perspective took place after the pilates exercises, when I simply did not want to get up from the floor after stretching. I was moving my eyes around invisible corners and suddenly, to my enormous surprise, which quickly turned into panic, I saw a huge maybug in the place where I keep my shoe boxes. For only a few seconds, I considered taking a photo, but then I decided to rescue him and put him on the windowsill. (Paulina)

Paulina disrupted her observation, driven by fright – and by compassion for the alien creature she discovered in her room. Instead of taking pictures or notes she took action to liberate the insect. By contrast, Aleksandra discovered the entire space anew, something that immobilized her and made her remain reflective and silent longer than she expected.

I paid attention to the decor of this room, the walls are painted in four different colours: light yellow, dark yellow, light turquoise and dark turquoise, which are intertwined in geometric patterns. The room has no door, only a wooden frame with traces of plaster being applied around it. The furniture is dark turquoise. A woman moves energetically around the kitchen. While washing the dishes, she is accompanied by the sounds of glasses hitting each other with walls and cutlery that ends up in a container by the sink. You can hear the sound of boiling water. The steam rising above the kettle settles on the bottom wall of the turquoise cabinet. It turns into tiny droplets of water dripping onto the constantly wet worktop. The number of washed glasses next to the sink is increasing, and they have also been joined by two jars (one for mayonnaise and one for cucumbers) and a slender transparent cup. Among the collection of these items, the red potato spoon attracts attention. There are not too many elements of this colour in the kitchen. You can also find it on a small salt shaker, the upper part of which is in the shape of a cat, or on several mugs with a Christmas pattern. Next to me is a chimney with a metal clock hanging from it. Not ticking. What is visible outside the window is reflected in the glass lid of the cooker raised and leaning against the wall. At this point, you can see snow falling in it. (Aleksandra)

Monika discovered something unexpectedly interesting, a potential connection between her and another person in her household as well as between herself and her curiosity to read different things.

I involuntarily made an observation during dinner at my family home, when we sat down in the living room, and I took a different seat at the table than before. I sat down in front of the bookshelf on which the books were placed, and I was slowly looking at the titles. I was aware of most of the titles we have, but I was honestly surprised to discover that our library contained a biography of a famous sportsman. For me personally, this is a new discovery, because I have never paid special attention to anyone in the house interested in the lives of celebrities. It gave me a new book to read, and who knows, I have to check other titles, maybe something interesting will catch my eye. (Monika)

Rain is taken for granted and not much relished in everyday life, by most of us and most of the time. However, when closely observed, it turned out to be surprising too:

I had the opportunity to see the first drops falling from the sky turn into rain, and it was then that I noticed the drops dancing on the concrete, bouncing off the heated surface. I have never before paid attention to what happens with a raindrop that ends its journey by hitting the ground, and it turns out that the moment it touches the surface is not the end of the journey, because at this point the reflecting drops jump and dance resembling thousands of rubber balls spilled out into the street. (Oliwia)

Several people discovered details hidden in the interior design which proved to be unexpectedly fascinating. Klaudia observed her bathroom and saw that it was almost monochromatic. And then she discovered something else – how such a simple décor changes with the light:

...the only colour that stands out from this trend is green in the plant standing by the sink. The floor is made up of wide tiles in gray – one of the simplest elements of the bathroom, compatible with the simplicity of cabinets and wall tiles. The wall behind the mirror, made of tiles with a characteristic texture, attracts attention. Their appearance, and therefore their reception, depend on the light (mainly artificial, as well as daylight)...The role of light and the visual effects that change with it is very important. (Klaudia)

The light appears in many responses. For Karolina it transported her into another reality – it was an epiphanic moment:

> In my house I covered something that I had not paid attention to so far. The sun's rays break through the panes of my window and pass through a curtain made of lace. Thanks to this phenomenon, a sun-painted stained-glass window is created on my wall. It makes me feel like I am not at home, but in some beautiful cathedral, at my own home, which I can visit and admire whenever the sun is shining. (Karolina)

Katja's observation starts with discovering the details but as she continues looking the image becomes dynamic, it unfolds into a little story:

> Tiled stove. A tile caught my attention...It has a dark brown colour. It beautifully reflects light from the window, especially when the sun is shining. The tiled drawing reflects a floral motif: flowers with four petals and stamens between them. Birch-like leaves begin to grow at the end of the petals. The drawing is framed in a square frame, in the corners of which, complementing the painting, are semi-circular lines resembling fern leaves. (Katja)

Klaudyna looks – and another of her senses wakes up. She hears a sound that has always been there, but which she failed to notice before:

> My studio is very small. I was convinced that I knew it intimately. But what did I discover there? New sounds – an old refrigerator that I didn't pay attention to before. I can hear it very clearly now. The sound resembles the noises of an old factory. They grow most intense in the evening when

I am trying to fall asleep. Then I hear them with redoubled strength. They bring to mind post-apocalyptic scenes taking place in the scenery like from the movie Blade Runner 2049. (Klaudyna)

Discovering a new element was interesting but also disturbing; it made it difficult for her to fall asleep for some time afterwards. It was much more pleasant for Amanda, who

turned off my computer, phone, radio and sat on the floor, exposing my face to the setting sun. It was a very interesting experience and just as I was about to finish it, I heard someone on the block next door playing the guitar. I've never heard this before, probably because there's music in my room most of the time. So I picked up my guitar quickly, joined into the music, and spent the afternoon that way (Amanda)

Olga was another person who discovered sound that she until then did not realize existed by careful looking.

Probably each of us knows the proverb 'children and fish have no voice'. Its validity can be debated, but now is not the time and place for it. But I have discovered something concerning it. There has always been an aquarium in my house (as long as I can remember). I have never had any particular interest in it because my dad takes care of it. However, while observing my surroundings, it intrigued me the most. Good heavens, how this aquarium is **loud**! This may seem strange, because the fish do not make any sounds. But the aquarium does: the hum of the filter, the sounds of the aerator and individual splashes! Was this an interesting experience, considering that I pass by the aquarium several dozen times a day! I even sit on the couch nearby and never noticed it. (Olga)

34

But beginning to hear by looking is not all that can happen when one concentrates. It can also convey

> [a] strange feeling, like being teleported but without moving anywhere. How is it even possible? I watched my room and then my gaze turned as if inwards. Who am I? What am I doing here? I mused for a moment what it is that is so strange with me, myself, right now. And then I realized – time slowed down. I was sitting there in slow motion time. (Patryk)

Looking and seeing marks the beginning of the journey in liminality. The imaginoscope helps to discover the role of the imagination. And it also brings the insight that there is a whole world waiting to be discovered beyond the confine of the solitary 'I'.

2. Encounter: Listening

2.1. Why listen to the Other?

The voyager, equipped with the imaginoscope, makes now a second stop in order to listen. She has learned to hear when intensely looking, but the imaginoscope, when applied to the ear instead of the eye, can do something even more ingenious: it can change the perspective of the observer.

When I was little, I enjoyed playing 'someone else'. I was imagining I was somebody else I knew personally or from TV. There was a magic door in our apartment block; if you went down into the basement and walked until one far end of the corridor, you came to an exit that led out into the yard. It was not quite on the level of the sidewalk, but slightly below. You see, my block was somewhat crooked, or, rather, the street was, it was located on a very gentle hillside, and one end was more deeply buried in the ground than the other. The other exit from the basement led to the common garage and that was much less interesting and rather mundane but the magical door was at the higher end. Almost no grown up ever used it; I think I never saw anyone else but me using it. And I made sure to never mention it to anyone, not even to my best friend. This is the first time I do so. The door opened just into one side; you could go out but not come in. It closed behind you with a soft sound: *oo-tah-kan*. And there you were – not you anymore, but someone else. There were times when you could plan whom to metamorphose into, but usually it was a surprise. I think it all began with one of my favourite TV series, *Randall and Hopkirk (Deceased)*, about private detectives Jeff Randall and Marty Hopkirk. The latter got murdered during an investigation but kept on returning as a ghost to help his partner, Jeff. The series fascinated me and Randall might have been the first character whose shoes I stepped into through the magic door. He was the only one who could actually see Hopkirk and I wanted to do that too. Of course, he appeared immediately and we had a lovely chat. Then I tested what it was like with other fictional characters and then came the real people: my lovely teacher Miss Barbro, Anna-Karin, a friend from school whom I much admired, who was riding horses, the fearful but rather splendid lifeguard of the swimming pool…I remember clearly the feeling after crossing the threshold. Everything changed: the way I moved, what I saw, how I felt about myself. When I was Anna-Karin I suddenly knew all about riding, it was a very embodied knowledge which made me move quite differently from what I was used to. I also felt an intense affiliation to horses and spent almost the entire duration of the spell thinking of how great they are and how gracefully they behave. The magic door was great fun and it worked as long as it was kept secret. But then we moved. I grew up and became a socially ambivalent teenager; I was fascinated by people and, at the same time, I was terrified of them. I realized I would never, ever be able to be someone else, not see the world as someone else saw it, not occupy space as someone else did. It was sobering – and heart-breaking. I was condemned to be – just me, and that was a cold and lonely feeling. I can only see the world through my own eyes and no matter how well I learn things, I'll never learn well enough to become somebody else. But the curiosity never left me, and a desire to see what it is like to be someone else kept coming back. There are as many worlds around as there are isolated observers and the walls between them are unsurmountable. The magic door is no longer there, even if I like to think that maybe, just maybe, it really existed a long time ago, when I was little and the world was full of things like magical elevators running sideways and buildings that changed their location in the night. However, there is a way of getting a glimpse of what is beyond the intractable walls between us: we can ask.

Invite a group of friends, colleagues or students to an informal setting. A café or your home works well, a classroom or conference room does not. Provide abundant coffee or tea for everyone. If your health allows you to drink alcohol, red wine can be a good idea for the occasion. Be a generous host. Abundance is a good context for sharing: food, stories and ideas. If possible assemble around a table or fireplace. Then ask your guests how exactly they see and perceive colours. Show them a painting, it does not have to be an original, of course, but the colours need to be quite clear. I like to use Lucio Fontana for this purpose but this is, of course, not a rule. For blue, Yves Klein may be more inspiring. Ask everyone to tell you what they see when they look at the colour in the painting; each person in turn. What exactly is, say, Klein blue, for each of them? What do they see, feel, what ideas, emotions and affects does it awaken in them? And, indeed, in yourself?

The imaginoscope contains a tool that can help us to learn about other people's lifeworlds without always having to organize symposions like this (even though they are delightful and should take place more often). It comes from ethnography and is known as ethnographic interview. These are a special member of the interview family. Interviews come in different shapes and styles. A well known type of interview is used for the collection of quantitative data and has to be conducted in a formally structured way, containing a predetermined set of questions and answers. This is known as the questionnaire. But this is not what shall be used in this chapter. Nor are all the other "question-and-answer" polls and consultations known from the media and from marketing research. The ethnographic interview is neither structured nor formalized. According to experienced researcher Barbara Czarniawska (1999) interview is 'more like a manipulated conversation, where the manipulation is acknowledged and accepted by both parties' (p. 5). The difference between the structured and unstructured interview is that the former is aimed at acquiring codable data and the latter – ethnographic – is all about getting a response from the other person which is as close to her or his life world as possible, without imposing any categories or ideas. In that it is like observation: the whole point is that the inquirer does not know and wants to learn something new from another person. It is about the art of listening to the things that the interlocutor is telling us. It is mutual conversation, however, one where one person listens more and the other talks more.

What is so unusual about talking? someone might ask. After all, we contemporary humans talk rather a lot. We chat incessantly: in person, on the phone, on social media. Much of modern work consists of chatting: the person at the till addressed the customer with a chatty line, the telemarketer called us to interrupt our dinner with his chat and a teacher, now as a hundred years ago, comes back home with a throat sore from talk. This is true and perhaps silence is much rarer for the contemporary urban dweller than making conversation. However, we are so rarely listened to; we listen so rarely. When we practise interviews in class, a number of my students describe the experience of actually being intensely listened to as a revelation. It has been described as something like sitting in a concert hall, like winning a prize and even like falling in love. It really makes a difference. I was asked by a quantitative colleague once whatever it is I do to make very busy people talk to me. Do I have any tricks? he wondered. I do not have any. People are busy and being interviewed is a gift of one's time. Many of our potential interviewees do not have the time to offer a complete stranger. Small wonder they often decline. Yet ethnographic interview, even if it takes tremendously more time than the standard questionnaire, is not just a gift of one's time to science. It is also something the interviewee received in exchange – attention, being listened to. They may initially tell us that they only have 10 minutes (much too short for an interview) but end up talking to us for hours. I have experienced this several times and so have many of my students. The feeling of being a centre of someone's attention cannot be shared, but some of the insights such a conversation brings can be communicated to others.

A fascinating book based in its entirety on an interview is anthropologist Ruth Behar's *Translated Woman* (1993). It is a portrait of a Mexican peasant woman, Esperanza. Esperanza was brought up in poverty, with no access to education and her life prospects are more limited than those of most of the intended readers, but her fate concerns us all; the book invites the reader to realize just how much it does so. The story told by the interviewee, Esperanza, and translated into the language of ethnography by Ruth, the interviewer, not only generates interest and empathy but also a sense of solidarity. Esperanza shares with Ruth – and with us – tales of suffering and hardship, of violence and loss, as well as of work and of religion. She talks of her mother and the tales her mother used to tell her. Of her father who was often violent when he was drunk. She had to start working when she was just 10, cleaning and cooking. Then she got married to an utterly irresponsible man and her struggles to make ends meet – and the abuse – continued. Six of her children died due to poverty and malnourishment. But Esperanza is no passive victim, she is a fighter. She turned in her aberrant husband to the law and began earning her life as a street peddler. But the book is not just an extensive life story of Esperanza; it is an interview, a conversation. It also contains the presence of the interviewer, Ruth, how the relationship between the two women developed, how there emerged trust despite the difference in class and privilege. Ruth remains deeply reflexive throughout the narrative: aware of her privilege and of the mirroring of two fates that take place during the encounter. It also contains a musing on academic identity, of what it means to listen ethnographically and then to write it down. Behar is profoundly aware that there are several layers of meaning and interpretation that cause losses in translation of lived experience and authenticity. But she does her best to understand as closely as she can – and to convey this understanding, of her interlocutor and of herself as listener, to the reader. By understanding Esperanza, Behar becomes more aware of the similarity and the difference between them, as women, as human beings, but also as partners in a conversation. At times the author seems to lose her discernment between researcher and researched, as if she started to over-identify with her interviewee. But maybe that is inevitable? After all, the subtitle of the book speaks of 'crossing the border' and that is exactly what is intended with it. Not unlike what I did with my magic door. To see what it is like to be someone else. But the book tries to take a step further: to cross yet another border by retelling the experience to others. Without the use of magic, only language can do that, however inadequately.

But we can try, we can do our best, thanks to the imaginoscope. Here are some guidelines of how to do an ethnographic interview which can be useful.

- Be open to what the interlocutor says, follow her lines of thought. You do not need a plan or questions prepared beforehand, just a general idea of what you would want to talk about. It is the interviewee who is the captain of this voyage, let her take you where she wishes. The more unexpected, usually the better.
- Do not pepper him with questions, allow him to take his time, to develop his narrative. Help him with that by asking questions pertaining to what he has said.
- Ask for examples, always ask for examples. Never be satisfied with abstract statements or declarations of opinion. It is the personal that allows us to perhaps catch a glimpse of the otherness of the Other.
- An ethnographic interview takes a long time. Usually not as long as Esperanza's story but rarely less than one hour. Ethnographers usually keep coming back to their interlocutors, asking them to continue their stories or fill in with new developments. If you are an amateur rather than professional ethnographer, then you do not need to be too rigorous with the collection of empirical material which would generate a theory, but it is still advisable to come back two or three times to the same person. Relationships develop in time and both talking and listening matures and gets better.
- Keep eye contact, be sensitive, react and respond but do not dominate the conversation.
- If you are a professional anthropologist you need to

preserve the material, by taking notes and recording the interview (of course after you get an approval from the interviewee). As an amateur ethnographer all you need to do is focus on the interlocutor.

- Ethnographers dedicate much care and attention to maintaining the anonymity of the interlocutors and to protecting their identity and privacy. We cannot, under any circumstances, endanger their safety and betray their trust. The relationship between ethnographer and her field is special, not unlike that between the doctor and his patient, or the priest and her parishioner. This must be cherished and respected. As amateur ethnographer, you are not a priest but more like, say, a wandering sage. Your integrity and honesty are of the utmost importance but you are unlikely to publish the results of your explorations. The simple rule is: be sincere, be respectful, never betray an interlocutor.

2.1. Practice: Listening

Imagine that filmmaker Jim Jarmusch[1] decided to make a short film showing a conversation between a randomly selected person and a famous public figure. Guess what, you were selected! The director sent you a letter of invitation, asking if you would like to take part in his new movie and, if so, whom you would like to talk to. He is able to procure any living interlocutor you would like to speak to. He also asks you what question you would like to ask your converser? There can only be one question.

Reflect:

- Whom would you choose to talk to?
- What question would you ask?

Write down the name and the question. Imagine what Jim Jarmusch would make of it. Try to see the clip before your mind's eye.

Imagining this situation makes a great preparation for listening. Many of my students dreamed about meeting an artist they respected, to learn about different aspects of their work. Some, like Olga, were interested in the organizational sides:

> If I had the opportunity to talk to any creator from the world of culture, I would choose Boris Eifman without hesitation. He is an undisputed authority in the world of dance and a choreographer known all over the world. If I could ask him just one thing, I would ask him how he chooses dancers for his Eifman Ballet (what key does he use?). (Olga)

Others wanted to learn about their life, how they manage to be creative in their societies, which are not always supportive of what they do and who they are:

> If I had the opportunity, I'd like to talk to Rei Kawakubo, an outstanding Japanese fashion designer and artist. I asked her where she draws inspiration for her unusual, original projects and the courage to design at her own discretion, not for the public. I would also ask how she has fared in Japanese society as a person breaking the pattern of a good wife and mother who should stay at home and instead chose to pursue an international career. What message would she like to convey to young women who above all want to develop professionally? (Anna Żur)

Quite a lot of students were particularly interested in the creative sides of their interlocutors' lives and some were looking for a possible area that could be used as a door. Dreams had such a potential.

I've always dreamed of talking to Ray Bradbury because he's

been my favourite writer for a long time. Unfortunately, he is no longer alive, so I will choose Dima Bonchinche, he is a Belarusian and Russian dancer and he is also the creator of Bonchinche voguing. I am interested in dancing and I love voguing: a relatively new genre of dance but with a great tradition already, with so many chapters and scenes [in many countries]. And I am very inspired by Dima. I would ask him about life, such as: 'What are you dreaming of?' (Volha Kavalskaya)

While many wanted to understand, to see, to empathize, some wanted to do something new, such as grab the opportunity to learn how to do something they would like to do better. Ania would have chosen to talk with the famous linguist Jerzy Bralczyk, in order to learn from him how to be a better conversationalist.

I think professor Jerzy Bralczyk would be a very interesting interlocutor. He is a person with whom you can learn a lot – not only in terms of linguistic correctness, but also in terms of the culture of expression itself. How to speak well and to be listened to? I think the answer to this question would be found in this interview. (Ania)

But a conversation with an artist can, perhaps, teach more than just a skill, however sophisticated.

I know that I have the whole world at my disposal, but I will stay in our Polish backyard. If I could, I would like to talk to Krzysztof Zanussi. He is a great influence for me, not only in the field of art, but also in the worldview and the whole of 'being a human'. But there is another reason. Mr Zanussi's voice is wonderful. I am a musician by education, and I love listening. And his voice is one of the most rare musical ones, when he talks it feels like music. I would ask him for advice for a young artist such as myself. My question for him would be: 'How to live?' He has vast experience. But if I could pose more questions, I would certainly ask which books made the greatest impression on him. I would ask if it is worth fighting for art and science, against all odds. I know his answer without even asking this question, but I am curious about the justification. Oh, there is an avalanche of questions in my mind that I would like to ask this amazing artist! (Maria)

An artist could also help to make sense of the current (at the time of writing) pandemic, not by providing a cure but by helping the interlocutor to take heart in a difficult situation.

Most of the people I really want to meet are unfortunately dead (ah, to talk to Susan Sontag about the disease metaphor in the COVID-19 age!). Would that get in the way of Jim Jarmusch? So I would invite Judith Butler to join the interview, with whom I would also like to discuss the current events. I would ask the author of Notes on the Performative Theory of Assembly how she sees resistance in times of isolation. I think that this question would give rise to a fiery and interesting discussion, which the director would not interrupt because it would be truly fascinating. (Joanna)

Some just wanted to be here and to listen. A conversation does not even always need specific questions, as Ania suggests.

I thought for a long time who I could talk to and finally chose – Hayao Miyazaki, because he is a director whose films accompanied me at every stage of my life. I have had contact with his work since I was a small child and it was he who awoke my love for Japan – language, culture and aesthetics.

Given the option to ask one question, I probably wouldn't ask any. I would just like to silently observe a traditional Japanese garden with him in the spring rain. Alternatively, I could ask 'Would we have some tea?' just in such a scenery. (Ania)

And, of course, a conversation would be able to reveal something of the other's world on the other side of the observation.

If there was an opportunity to interview a person of my choice from the world of culture, it would surely be the leader of the [musical] group the Swans – Michael Gira... So far I have been to two of his solo concerts and two with the Swans. Each of them was a truly mystical experience – Gira on stage becomes a real shaman. After the last concert in Warsaw, watching him and listening to conversations with fans, I got the impression that he was tired of signing CDs, saying thanks and answering questions. This is just my observation, but at times his facial expressions seemed to reveal his weariness. So the question struck me – is it very exhausting to have an audience? Or energizing? What is it like? That is what I would ask him about this experience, it would be a confrontation of my observations with his own position. And I would hope to hear what it is like to share his works with us. How does the audience affect him? (Marianna)

The other's point of view can also pertain to something more concrete. People sometimes say things that are inspiring but puzzling, maybe artists especially have this custom. A conversation is a possibility to inquire, find out what is behind such a statement.

I'd like to interview Martha Graham. Martha once said, 'When a dancer is dancing, the ground beneath him is sacred.' The way they were disappointing and kept their eyes on sleep. (Aneta)

Some people have seen and experienced things that are beyond the grasp of most of us. It would be infinitely interesting to find out something not just about themselves but about the world, such as they see it.

Col. Chris Hadfield is a Canadian retired astronaut who made a name for himself with his cover of the song Space Oddity by Bowie. The cover was so amazing (and hence its viral character) that it was made on the International Space Station by Hadfield[2].

At the very end of a 1993 interview with CBC News Canada, when Hadfield was taking his first steps at NASA and the first of his three expeditions to the ISS was just ahead of him, Hadfield said: 'I guess from the outside I look much like I'm in control but I'm just as confused about life in general and the reason we're all here as anybody else.' His statement raises my questions to him: After so many years and after such extraordinary experiences as being in outer space and the opportunity to look at the world (literally) from above, from a distance, from a perspective that for many is only an imagination, is his world view still as confused and unclear as it was 27 years ago? What has changed in his perspective? What is the meaning of life? (Olga)

Some students saw this conversation as a possibility for an (imagined) exchange. An experienced person can offer important reflections on his life. The inquirer can identify with his younger self and learn something useful for her own path.

I would invite Paolo Sorrentino. He is an Italian director

whose fantastic films always carry a lot of weight. Watching his films, I believe that maybe the artist struggles with aging, maybe longs for his lost youth, as this theme is recurrent throughout his productions. 'If you were to advise your younger self, what would you advise him to spare him from suffering?' – that would be my question to him. (Agnieszka)

Sometimes what drives the interviewer is sheer curiosity, perhaps of an elusive or secretive interviewee. Then even asking a seemingly naïve question can be extraordinarily alluring.

I would choose Milan Kundera because he was my first 'literary love' from my teenage years. However, what I would like to ask him is a more difficult question - as far as I know, Kundera has not been interviewed for over a quarter of a century, so all the questions that come to mind seem too trivial or pseudo-intelligent to me. Maybe I would just ask him 'are you happy?' – although this also seems to be a naive question (Martyna)

If I had the opportunity, I'd like to talk to Banksy – I think it would be an amazing honour, considering he is one of the most mysterious and recognizable artists. I would ask him the same question he asked potential buyers of his works – why does art matter? (Monika)

Some would take the opportunity to talk with the director himself. Then they would try to find out what feelings his art evokes in him.

In this imaginary story, I'd like to talk to...Jim Jarmusch! He is one of my beloved creators and this is what I would like to talk to. One question I could ask him would be: What is a movie for you? You can reach various interviews in which the creators talk about the fields they deal with, but I would like to see this almost elusive change on the director's face when he thinks about what the type of art he creates is for him. (Natalia)

Dominika would explore some of the boundaries between art and life – something that is fascinating for her and what also seems to be strongly present in Jarmusch's films.

Has it ever happened that one meeting with a stranger, just a few random moments, a few exchanged words (perhaps over coffee and cigarettes, on the train or in a taxi) turned out to be extremely significant, contributed to changes in his life or at least for some reason still not gives him peace. (Dominika)

Yuliia finds the imaginary conversation irresistible. She, too, would interview the director himself to find out more about conversation itself.

Even if you hadn't sent the film by Jim Jarmusch today, I would have chosen this genius for the interview. This is my favourite director who forces you to breathe to the rhythm with the characters of his films, makes you feel alive, even when he talks about the dead (although I'm afraid to talk to such people). I don't think it makes sense to ask a director what meaning he gives to specific events in the movies. Because a good director, in my opinion, allows each of us to look for our own meanings in what we see. I just love him for the fact that he does not give ready-made recipes and formulas, does not say axioms and does not impose anything. On the other hand, it makes you think, reflect on the important thing, look at life from a different angle – often unexpected. By appealing to the viewers' experience and their imaginations, he introduces into the game details that can often be the main characters in movies. What would I ask him? I prefer to conduct an ethnographic interview without any prepared questions. The main topic of this conversation will be the choice of a creative path, just creativity itself. Rather, I plan to follow the director's thoughts, 'asking' during the conversation about what during his life helped him find the answer to the questions 'What do I want?', 'Where to go?' I chose this format because for me it is important not so much to get answers to my questions, but to get to know the way of thinking of this beautiful human. And I would conduct this conversation, for example, in a taxi – a place where people usually don't give thought to conversations and quickly forget about them...other people, but certainly not Jarmusch! The films Night on Earth, Coffee and Cigarettes are just about such important accidental conversations. And Paterson – about the important thoughts of the bus driver. A lot of people are wondering what the bus driver is thinking about?

Here are some possible questions (if there is room for them during the conversation):

'What do you think about when you are drinking coffee?'

'What question has recently appeared in your head and which you have not found an answer to?'

'What would you like to talk about with a stranger in a cafe?'
'What if you became a fish?'

'Coffee or cigarettes?' (Yuliia Savytska)

Most of my students chose interlocutors from the art world, perhaps in part because they were all interested in the arts, and in part because of the proposed setting. After all, Jarmusch's conversers were artists. But a few chose politicians or businessmen. These conversations tended to be dramatically different from the citations above. The interviewers no longer wished to learn, to explore, but, rather, to force the other side to listen, as in Karina's response:

> If I could ask anyone on Earth, I would like to ask Jeff Bezos
> if he is aware of how many people he could help with his
> money to just survive, just make a living, without losing
> the comfort of life he has at the moment. I would ask if he
> ever considered what it is like for someone to work in one of
> his warehouses. If he would want to spend his life like that.
> (Karina)

This exercise concerns an imagined conversation, not a real one.
It is not in any way my intention to discourage the readers from
having real dialogues and conducting interviews with actual
persons; quite the opposite. However, this book is a quest, a
journey in liminality, to be made in between the imagination
and the world out there. And for this purpose an imagined
conversation with a famous person in Jim Jarmusch's film is
how I propose to use the imaginoscope to prepare to listen. The
exercise directs narrative attention towards otherness, what
experiences certain knowledgeable others have that one would
like to acquire, what energies one would wish to soak up and
test, just as I did when I was crossing my magical door.

3. Language: Mythical tales

3.1. The usefulness of myths

An imagined conversation with an artist can help to lend
energies to use in the quest for insight somewhat outside of
the mundane world (but not in opposition towards it) but it
does not quite help to find a voice of one's own to use in this
liminal domain. We need to put the imaginoscope to yet another
use – apply it to the tongue and bring about a language of the

Imagination.

There is a language that fits very well the realm located on the boundaries of the known and the unknown, the sacred and the profane. It is the language of myth. It is more than just what we call language in our everyday speech: it provides a rich symbolism and a narrative thrust which can propel the narrator and her audience towards the Grail. According to American mythologist Joseph Campbell (1988a), myth is a type of narrative where *truth* is something different than in a realistic tale. Whether something really happened or not is insubstantial. The truthfulness of a mythical tale refers, instead, to a deeper reality of the soul, spirit or the imagination, such as William Blake understood it, not fantasy but 'the real & eternal World of which this Vegetable Universe is but a faint shadow & in which shall live in our Eternal or Imaginative Bodies, when the Vegetable Mortal Bodies are no more'. (2019; p. 797). This domain is both the reality and the human capacity to perceive it. Myths unlock the human capacity to address this reality by offering a way of perceiving and talking about

> matters fundamental to ourselves, enduring essential principles about which it would be good for us to know; about which, in fact, it will be necessary for us to know if our conscious minds are to be kept in touch with our own most secret, motivating depths. In short, these holy tales and their images are messages to the conscious mind from quarters of the spirit unknown to normal daylight consciousness, and if read as referring to events in the field of space and time – whether of the future, present, or past – they will have been misread and their force deflected, some secondary thing outside then taking to itself the reference of the symbol, some sanctified stick, stone, or animal, person, event, city, or social group (Campbell, 1988a, p. 24).

This is possible because myths have the ability to connect the external, mundane reality with the internal, spiritual reality, by giving a meaning to the liminality in between. They are able to do that because they are powerful metaphors, which direct attention towards something beyond themselves and, at the same time, use familiar images and plots (Campbell, 1988b). They tell stories of heroes and heroines equipped with magical powers, divinities altering shape, people encountering angels. A rationalist indulgently nods his head: how do these silly people use their logical facilities? They believe anything! But that is not how these stories are intended to be read. Literal readings exist but they are misreadings rather than typical ways to approach myth. A skillful understanding is, however, not about disregarding the narrative as a kind of fairy tale for grown-ups. The goddess Demeter mourns her lost daughter Kore every winter season and this really happens on a collective emotional plan: when autumn starts giving way to winter and nature turns away from us, grows cold and more contemplative than exuberant. Her usually vivid colours are replaced by the traditional colours of mourning: black of the West, white of the East. The days grow shorter and the darkness at times overpowers us. But then everything changes with the arrival of spring. It explodes with energy, colour and light, indeed – it springs. There is a time just before it happens, when we feel a massive change approaching.

Ides of March
There's a suggestion of a smell of spring.
Not quite of blossom, fresh
sprouting; rather, a premonition
enclosed in the response
of earth to the step,
the way the dust stirs
the breath,

the afterimages in the shape of white swirls
formed by the tang
of sunshine.

Yes, it can happen.
Redemption and Revolution (Monika Kostera, 2016, p. 73)

We know this is not strictly a story of real-life events, happening out there in physical space. Something is happening there: the astronomical vernal equinox, when the tilt of the Earth towards the sun increases, and the length of daylight quickly intensifies, marks a period of biological events such as the blossoming of a range of plants, activities of animals, changes in the weather. But something is also happening in our minds and hearts: a sense of approaching 'redemption and revolution'. This mindset is not individual in spring; it is shared by many, human and non-human inhabitants of our planets. This is the domain of the imagination which Blake spoke of. We can feel we share the less visible and less scientifically expressible events and moods. They are at least as significant as the external ones. Of course they can be narrated with a language of biology, medicine, psychology, but most of us would probably agree that this is not all there is to spring. Some, like myself in the poem cited above, resort to poetry to try to express how they feel in a form that would be intelligible for others. But we may want to indulge in a shared mood and meaning of the approach of spring using the language of myth: in art, song, storytelling, ceremonies, festivals. The story of Demeter moves us and unites us: the goddess of nature is rejoicing in the approaching return of her beloved daughter from the Underworld where she dwells in wintertime as wife of its ruler and so, its queen. The story touches something in the human soul that is not just about individual psychological well-being or our appetite for fantastic tales. It does so because it contains constructs that often turn up as powerful cultural symbols, known as archetypes.

As I have explained in the Introduction, archetypes are not 'things' or ideas, but slots in our collective imagination that 'attract' certain contents. Swiss psychiatrist Carl Gustav Jung (1968) depicted them as reminiscent of riverbeds: slots to be filled by narratives, such as – in particular – mythical tales. Imagination works through the use of stories and images based on archetypical material. This is where inspiration comes from; these images provide storytellers, artists and mystics with a language to express the otherwise all but inexpressible. Joseph Campbell (1988) observed how certain motifs tend to be repeated in myths, legends, traditional stories, as well as in private fantasies and dreams. The hero in traditional legends gets a call to adventure, embarks upon the journey receiving supernatural help and encountering guardians of the threshold. The transformation begins: a path of challenges and lessons. At some point the hero faces a particularly difficult juncture, a major crisis, perhaps death. After that he emerges transformed, possessing a greater understanding, and receives a divine gift which he carries back home to share with his co-villagers. This plot template is known as the monomyth or the hero's journey (Campbell, 2012). This template can be found in the classical myths of Heracles, in the tales of the knights of the round table, and in modern sagas such as *The Lord of the Rings* and *Star Wars*.

Archetypes are universal in time and space and shared by humanity across eras and cultures. They never become obsolete with the passage of time but remain vivid and constantly inspire new ideas and interpretations. Consider the myth of Gaia: the goddess occupied an important place in the narrative pantheon of Antiquity and attracts much attention today as the symbol of a living planet. The way we relate to those tales changed (from faith to environmental awareness) and so has Gaia herself: from chthonic primordial divinity to living dynamic biosphere. Even though both archetypes and stereotypes are widespread, they are, in other respects, each other's opposites. Stereotypes tell us 'what things are really like' to replace conscience and pacify attention. They offer an easy judgement that makes it possible to encounter complex events and persons with a simplified script, on autopilot. Archetypes are endlessly multifaceted, ambivalent, never easy to judge or classify. They wake up human consciousness, sometimes in an overpowering way, evoke strong feelings, including uncomfortable ones such as mourning, wrath or ecstatic joy, often several simultaneously. They hold great power, cannot easily be manipulated by human beings and provide an inexhaustible source of inspiration and motivation. They are narrative pathways connecting us to something much larger than our individual selves and fates – a language containing

> forms we use for assigning meaning [which] are historical Categories that reach back into the mists of time – a fact we do not take sufficiently into account. Interpretations make use of certain linguistic matrices that are themselves derived from primordial images. From whatever side we approach this question, everywhere we find ourselves confronted with the history of language (Jung, 1980, p. 32-33).

The language and symbolism provided by archetypes makes it possible to compose mythical stories that fulfil a fundamental role in human sensemaking. Psychologist Jerome Bruner (1990) argues that storytelling is the most important human way of making sense of reality and communicating it. In the terms of Edgar Morin's (1990) philosophy of complexity, this is a process of negentropy. Negentropy is an idea derived from thermodynamics, referring to the regeneration process that allows living systems to preserve their complexity and remain alive. Living systems are open, they communicate with their environment: receive from it things like nourishment, energy and information, and send, in turn, their contribution or a product into the environment. In contrast, closed systems exchange nothing with their surroundings. Like stones, they are cut off and dead, but also – very stable, nothing much happens with them over time. Open systems are all the time at risk of losing more than they gain. In Edgar Morin's words, 'the rules of organization of the living are not those of equilibrium, but of disequilibrium, caught up or compensated for, a stabilized dynamism' (p. 31). This dynamism, called negentropy, enables open systems to resist their loss of energy and increasing entropy – dissipation and disorder leading to death. It is rare and precious: tiny sparks of life in an immense space of chaos. I believe that stories, and especially myths, are important human strategies of finding and mobilizing negentropy. Stories present us with sensemaking tools such as plots, characters, settings and themes that help not just to pass on information or knowledge but direct our attention, provide ways of ordering the infinite complexity of things and processes around us. Myths are even more powerful ordering devices, because they help to control the unknown and impossible to know, they – as if – plunge into raw chaos and bring back bits of meaning that can be used to expand our life world, to make it more complex without a loss of order and meaning. In other words, myths not only prevent entropy and chaos, but are tools that enable us to turn fragments of chaos into elements of living order. Even if mythical plots of persons gaining immortality on Earth are not true factually, they perform exactly that function for roles, values and ideas that help us to fight back death as the large living system of humanity.

Myths are stories that connect two realities: the internal and external (Campbell, 1988b). They can refer to sacred domains, placed more in the internal reality of the spirit, soul, perhaps also supernatural beings. But they need not be only stories of the sacred; there are many profane myths, placed in contexts that remind us of our everyday lives. Organization theorist Yiannis

Gabriel uses myth in his narratives of managers, workplaces and workers, addressing explicitly the liminal sphere between external and internal spaces. In the modern retelling of the myth of Odysseus and the Sirens, Gabriel (2020) shreds light on some aspects of the social sphere that the COVID-19 epidemic brought upon us: social distancing, isolation and the silencing of public spaces. Odysseus of the classical Homeric myth undertakes a long and perilous journey home from the Trojan war, as depicted in the Odyssey, and encounters many challenging events and dangerous creatures, among them the Sirens. These half-birds and half-women are chthonic divinities who lure sailors to their deaths with their enchanting song. The sailors fall into a trance and their boats get wrecked against the rocky coast of the Sirens' Island. The enchantress Circe advises Odysseus to put beeswax in his and his men's ears so they can ignore the Sirens' song and safely pass by their land. However, Odysseus is curious, he cannot deprive himself of this extraordinary musical experience. He orders his sailors to use the wax, whereas he himself refrains from any dulling of his sense of hearing. Instead, he asks to be tied to the mast and not to untie him until they pass out of earshot of the mesmerizing music. Gabriel first offers Franz Kafka's re-reading of the story, in which he switches archetypes from the hero to the aspiring sage. In this tale Odysseus blocks his ears and ties himself to the mast. The Sirens fall silent when the ship passes by and their silence is much more lethal than their song. But they see the calm expression on Odysseus' face – he probably does not know that they have fallen silent, or he is pretending not to know it, thus protecting himself from divine wrath. This is a different Odysseus, who possesses both placidity and humility. Gabriel explains that Kafka's version is a story of misperceptions. The hero misperceives and so do the Sirens. There is an unknowing underpinning both, somewhat serene and quite respectful. For Kafka silence is truly more dangerous than enchanted music, because 'it leaves us alone with our demons, our dark fantasies and our dark thoughts against which we seek noise to sweep them away' (2020, p. 321). Then Gabriel's narrative offers yet another retelling of the myth, in which it is we who at the same time are seduced and misperceive. We are seduced by the hero's self-containment, serenity and his narcissism; his ability to sail by 'blissfully, unharmed through a sea of silent killers, not unlike today's COVID-19' (p. 326). The silence of the Sirens is lost hope and the degradation of contemporary culture. Indeed, '[t]he silence of the Sirens stands for a culture that denies music its critical and subversive potential, turning it into the latest opium of the people' (p. 327). Ultimately, with COVID-19, the silence becomes a portent of alienation and death, a forced isolation and the immobility of the lockdown. Deprived of the ordinary noise, people seek what clatter they can invite into their private space: the news, the entertainment, the cacophony of social media. We fear the imposition of silence upon us because we know that it threatens to unleash our darkest fears. Anything seems better than allowing it to befall. Many people actively invite the loud voices of demagogues vying for power and promising simple solutions to increasingly complex problems in order to avoid the pain of silence. And yet this is not the whole story, Gabriel reveals at the end of his narrative. Kafka's Ulysses (Odysseus) has, after all, succeeded in sailing serenely past the silent Sirens. Doing this he may be re-read once again, as an archetype of hope. Perhaps this silent serenity directed at what is beyond the current moment can 'offer us a symbolic way of coping with pain and anxiety and open up bright windows with positive images for a revitalized future' (p. 329).

Now, let's spin this tale further. Thanking Homer, Kafka and Gabriel for the ride, let us pause and let the tale unravel for each of us, wherever it takes us. Imagine the scene: Odysseus sailing safely past the Sirens' Island, his sailors hard at work with the sails, the oars; the smells of the Mediterranean that have become so omnipresent that they do not notice them. The sea roars. The Sirens – do they sing or are they silent? The horizon then broadens, the danger is over. The men lay aside the oars and wipe away the sweat. Someone fetches an amphora with precious fresh water and they pass it around – they have earned it. One of them approaches Odysseus and starts to unbind his arms, while his companions take out the wax from their ears. They relax, they look around…what do they see? What happens now, what do they hear? What does Odysseus say to them and what do they answer? As with Kafka's and Gabriel's versions of the myth, you can follow the narrative thrust that appears for you, in any direction it takes you. It may be a story, or an image, it may of course also be music.

Tales and vision unraveling like this, driven by the creative impulse, are a common consequence of the presence of myth. In Yiannis Gabriel's story there is more than just a retelling of an ancient narrative. The story contains references to numerous other retellings, not just Kafka's story, and a number of artists who found the tale inspiring throughout different ages. There are strong connections between myth and art. British historian of religion Karen Armstrong (2006) explores this affinity: both can transform the human psyche, and both do so not by persuasion or discursive methods but by immediate experience. The role of neither of them has been limited to attempts at explaining how the material world works. Armstrong argues that they live in the human psyche, accompany us on life's journey.

The whole point of using myth as inspiration is to let oneself be guided by the creative impulse it offers. So, naturally, there can be no rules of how to use the imaginoscope to release the language of myth. However, the simple guidelines that follow may, perhaps, be useful for the learner, if applied openly and non-dogmatically.

- Choose a mythical tale that you feel attracted to in this

very moment of your life. Read a classical narrative. Look for later retellings in stories, poems, visual art. Take your time. Mythical thinking is not about the finding of effective solutions, but about allowing yourself to be taken out of your everyday realistic rhythms and placed in a domain of reverie. Myth is slow, adapt to its paces.

- Use your imagination to connect with the setting of the mythical tale. Leave the plot aside for a moment and dwell on the background. Use what you feel like using from the versions you have read or looked at. Fill in the rest with your own reveries and ideas. Where is the tale placed? What are the details of the place: what does it smell like? What does the light look like? How does it make you feel? Study the images of the persons, human and non-human (especially the supporting characters) in your mind in the same way, try to visualize them and do not force any narrative upon them: let them speak and act for themselves.

- Do not necessarily force a conclusion on the story that is unraveling. Some myths do not have a conclusion. Profane stories do, but myths are different. Sometimes they have an ending (final or temporary) and sometimes they just go on, like an endless yarn to spin. The more puzzling it is, the better it fulfils its role of provider of symbols of the unknown.

- Don't think of yourself as author of the tale, rather, as a bard catching visions and ideas and putting them into a story or a song.

3.2. Practice: Spinning mythical tales

Imagine that one evening, when you are walking home through a largely empty city, you encounter a vivid and strikingly beautiful character talking on his mobile phone. You stop and stare. This is incredible, isn't it? You just know who this is, even before you notice his winged sandals. He is irresistibly charismatic, gloriously androgynous, and there is a lightness about his every move. You realize you are staring, which is rather rude, and so you quicken your steps to walk away. But he looks right at you and addresses you in a soft yet strangely authoritative voice:

'I'm chatting with Socrates. Do you want to have a word? You can ask him one question. Just one, mind you!' he smiles lightly and commandingly at the same time.

What would you ask?

My students were happy to grab the opportunity. Some, appreciating that this is an occasion to jump into a never-ending story, would ask his advice for contemporary times.

The question I would ask Socrates is: Is your famous maxim, 'I know that I know nothing', losing its relevance in the 21st century? I would ask him this because in the age of the Internet and many 'scientifically confirmed' theories, often fake, I do not know if we really believe we still know something anymore. I think that Socrates could have extremely interesting thoughts on this matter. (Aneta)

Indeed, what would he do equipped with modern IT technology?

I once read that Socrates did not regard writing very highly, he believed that the spoken word was the key. He did not write down his views and teachings, he delivered them in the streets. Therefore, I would ask Socrates if he had lived in the present day, in the age of the Internet, would he still not use the written text? Would he remain a traditionalist and continue teaching in the streets, or, maybe, would he rather become a Youtuber and convey his wisdom to a wider audience in videos? Would he start creating and publishing written posts in the Internet? (Edyta)

Has something changed beyond his wisdom or is there a philosophical answer to this change in the mores?

I would ask Socrates if humility is as important today as it was in the years of his life because one of the philosopher's most famous quotes, 'I know that I know nothing', would today be perceived as weakness. (Pawel)

We, humanity, still know nothing, and yet, if knowledge is to be found in questions and answers – are we able to learn?

Although wisdom and knowledge are of great value, they are to some extent subjective. That is why they have often been, are and will be a source of various misunderstandings and conflicts, bringing with them various negative consequences (as exemplified by the fate of Socrates himself). The above question is certainly a difficult one, but I am sure Socrates would have found the right answer. (Grzegorz)

Paulina wanted help with knowing herself.

Who am I? I would ask this question because Socrates was able to open people's eyes to what surrounds them, and also to look inside himself to understand his nature. (Paulina)

Several would ask for pretty straightforward – if not very simple – advice on happiness and truth.

So I would ask 'How to be happy in life, what is the recipe for happiness?' Of course, I realize that there is no single answer to this question, happiness means something different for everyone. I would like to know what the Greek philosopher's response would be, what happiness is for him and what is the best way to achieve it according to him. (Aleksandra)

I would ask Socrates how to live in order to pursue the truth. Is there a golden mean? Does it lead to the truth? I wonder...and he knows, I think. (Oliwia)

In today's world:

I would ask Socrates about how to find an inner balance that would give warmth and inner peace. I would ask this question because I am constantly looking for answers and it seems to me that in today's times of 'movement' and 'rush', in the times of technology, humans lose themselves and their inner balance. What, under such conditions, can help us to find a sense of warmth and peace, regardless of external factors? Who knows, maybe he would give me a hint for my quest...(Anastassiya)

A few would grab the opportunity to get to know the great philosopher better. And what better way to do that than talking about books? Also, profiting from the mythical character of the meeting, time can be deprived of its absolute power over human knowing.

'Socrates, what is your favourite book written in the last hundred years?'
I believe that a favourite book says a lot about a person, their values, insights and dreams. I am curious what Socrates would say. Socrates was not a proud person, he did not extort the values of the things he knew. But he enjoyed reading and using texts written by other scholars. He believed that wisdom was born of interaction with people and their texts. I wonder what I would learn from Socrates' favourite contemporary book – what wisdom would it come from? (Joanna)

Chris wanted to learn more about the human being Socrates actually was:

> I wanted to ask Socrates one question since I studied archaeology. Well, in one message that I cannot find in the depths of the Internet, I found a report that Socrates (during his military service) was unmatched in both fighting and drinking wine. I would love to ask Socrates if this was the case. (Chris)

But wisdom is not just a thing of the mind. It is also a thing of the heart. Weronika, noting that Plato had limited his narrative of Socrates to just the first area, probably had distorted the whole picture. So she would

> ask who he was so in love with and how things turned out. What was the truth about Xanthippe? Was Plato just jealous and distorted her image? Anyway, even in Plato's rendering of Socrates' words, we can find sparse statements referring to feelings, for example, 'For those who suffer even the smallest joy is happiness', 'Whoever has a good spouse will be happy, whoever has a bad spouse will become a philosopher' or 'A loving heart will never grow old.' I think that none of this has grown outdated. How does one get a wisdom loving heart? That I would like to ask Socrates' wisdom of the heart. (Weronika)

Several wanted to take advantage of his expert powers as predictor of the future. Maybe he knows what will happen?

> I would ask Socrates how the coronavirus epidemic will affect our future lives and how long will the 'state of emergency' last? This is a question that many people ask themselves at the moment. It has so many and so fundamental consequences to

the world and our lives. Socrates could perhaps know the answer, some thoughts and predictions to share with me. (Ola)

Adriana had a similar question, and added:

How do I bring the world back to normal (and what normal? something similar to before the pandemic? Something else?) once the COVID-19 crisis is under control? (Adriana)

War and peace is another major issue that the students wished to address.

Why, I would ask, are today's country leaders not wise enough to resolve international conflicts without weapons? I would ask him such a question, because I come from a country where, from 2014, there is a constant war ongoing. And for the time being, no solution has yet been found in this conflict. (Yana)

Is there a way of making people see, making them aware, doing something before it is too late?

I would ask Socrates how, in times of the climate crisis and epidemic, to get some people to think about their actions and their effects. A lot of terrible things are happening right now, and a lot of people just don't seem to notice them, as if deciding not to see them, act without taking these ominous catastrophes into account. Hence my question to Socrates. I often do wonder how to shake people out of ignorance. They live in it, they don't seek knowing. (Katarzyna)

Eliza holds similar fears and would also ask about remedies to the crisis, but her question is angled somewhat differently.

It is amazing that despite the fact that so many years have passed, many issues raised by this philosopher are extremely accurate in the 21st century. I think because of his wisdom, I would ask for advice that is quite significant in the present situation. I think that regardless of other matters and values that are of great importance to us on a daily basis, the current situation in the world has completely re-evaluated our actions, plans, goals and dreams. Fear for tomorrow and uncertainty are two issues that preoccupy almost every citizen of the world. I would ask Socrates how to unite people, so that they would put aside their own aims and pursuits for a common good. We need a lot of patience, cooperation, new solutions, humility and listening to the advice of the sages to survive the global crisis and be able to come out of it unscathed; let the Earth regain her health. (Eliza)

In similar vein, a number of students asked about the future of teaching and learning (how can we learn something in today's world?) and about the future of leadership (is it possible to be a wise leader? Or maybe can a sage such as himself be persuaded to take upon himself to perform the role of leader?). Some inquired about further, eternal wisdom. Were there any conclusions beyond the ephemeral human timeline?

When you were alive, you said, 'I know that I know nothing.' What do you know now, after your death? Socrates taught people by asking questions and constantly sought the truth. He was especially interested in the human soul. So now I would like to ask him a question about the soul. Does it know the truth better than the body? (Anna)

Whereas contemporary science often shies away from the issue of human consciousness, Socrates would not. Karolina hopes he would point her in some direction she failed to find during her university studies:

How do you know that you know nothing? (Karolina)

Indeed, Socrates, the wisest among men, would know, maybe, what to do when the world is ending.

I would ask him what to do when everything we believed in and into which we have been putting all of our energies has come to an end. Everything I thought I was striving to achieve. The planet – falling apart. (Julia)

Finally, there is one more important question and it concerns the myths themselves, as well as their readership.

I would ask Socrates why myths are made to look nice and tidy when edited into stories for kids? I got my first book of Greek myths from my parents when I was in kindergarden. Then, in secondary school, I read [a popular edition of myths for children by] Parandowski. Then, when I was about to graduate, my Dad handed me a book by Robert Graves and announced that it would change my view of myths forever. And so it did, of course for the better. I discovered how rich and complex they were! But so are the Brothers Grimm fairy tales. Why are, then, myths so often made sugary sweet and polite? Dear Socrates, answer me, why do adults do that to them, thus tearing them off from the truth? (Patrycja)

This is indeed a good question. Sanitized versions of myths, addressed to children, are not just an instance of adaptation of these complex stories for a specific market segment. This market segment happens to be an important part of who we are, our humanity. We have all been children and childhood tends to stay with us as something important and cherished:

even if we do not necessarily have to agree with psychoanalysis that it lies at the root of all our adult complexes, then most of us tend to preserve and value our childhood memories. Myth in an infantilized version is not just simplified but sterilized. It separates mythical complexity and a child's imagination from each other. And yet myth and childhood belong together.

Now use the imaginoscope to answer all these questions that the students posed. It will help you to hear the answer that Socrates gave each of them.

4. Involvement: Hanging around with your inner child

4.1. The soulfulness of the child

If you put the imaginoscope close to your heart, something there will spring alive: your inner child. Children are able to observe the external and the internal reality with seriousness and involvement – an ability which is often lost in adulthood. In the well-known fairy tale 'The Emperor's New Suit' by Hans Christian Andersen (2016), there once lived an emperor who loved to dress stylishly and expensively. In his pursuit of fashion, he hires two swindlers, who promise to deliver the latest epitome of vogue and taste. Only clever people are able to see these exquisite garments, the swindlers assure him, fools cannot. The emperor pays them lavishly and in advance, and equips them with the finest silks and gold-cloths, and the swindlers set up their looms and get to work. A number of high officials check up on their progress and fail to see anything materializing on the looms but, afraid that they would be regarded as fools by the others, pretend to be in awe of the effect of the swindlers' work. When the clothes are finished – but in reality simply do not exist – the dishonest craftsmen pretend to dress the emperor in his new attire and he, too, pretends to see and appreciate it. Everyone else says it is an outfit of outstanding beauty, so he does not want to admit to his failure to see anything at all. 'Dressed' this way, he sets off for a procession in the city. All the inhabitants cheer and admire his new clothes, because everybody else does and no one wishes to stand out and appear foolish. Finally, a small child looks at the emperor parading naked along the street and exclaims: 'But he has nothing on at all' (p. 1071). And indeed, everyone sees that quite clearly now, including the emperor himself – the new outfit does not exist.

Wim Wenders' now classical film *Wings of Desire* (1987) begins with a recitation of Peter Handke's poem, 'Song of childhood'. It presents the child as deeply observant, immersed in everything around her.

When the child was a child,
it didn't know that it was a child,
everything was soulful,
and all souls were one. (Handke, 1987)

The child sees and wants things to be what she sees in them. A brook is a river, a river is a torrent. She asks excellent questions: 'Why am I me, and why not you?' She wants to know when time begins and where space ends. She understands that the boundaries between life and dream are far from obvious, far from given; in certain circumstances, transmissive. She loses many of these abilities as she grows up. But certain things remain: the taste of apples, walnuts, bread; the longing for even higher mountaintops, for greater cities, the awaiting of the first snow. Not everything is lost.

Wim Wenders' film conveys this sense of quivering. Its opening scenes portray a hand writing Handke's poem, a view of the sky, an angel high up watching over the big city, Berlin, and children's faces turned towards the angelic figure, seemingly invisible to all the other passers-by. As every human city, Berlin has angels watching over it, tuning in to people's thoughts, trying to care for them. But they are invisible to adults and only the children can see them.

Children are rarely bored when they are left more or less alone by adults to explore the world. Children, mystics and, indeed, ethnographers are able to focus on what is unique and concentrate on the moment, before they categorize away the uniqueness, before they name the unnamed. For children it is a given, obvious ability: this is how they learn new things. There is no greater pleasure than doing this. Curiosity and imagination overlap, they follow the same rhythms, sending out the child on so many irresistible quests: to explore the attic in the old country house she is visiting with her parents, to investigate every square centimetre of the basement in her apartment block, to discover a secret garden in the back yard of the grocery store...Children are bored silly only when forced to follow adults' paths and clues: when they are told to attend family dinners. Given an honest chance, most of them prefer an old discarded kettle to play with than an expensive toy. The toy is great but just for a day or two. The kettle is a secret item that is worth coming back to and retrieving over and over again. The toy is a shiny surface. The kettle is a multi-layered thing with roots in dimensions where adults do not tread.

Unless they are mystics. Or ethnographers. It is possible to see the infinity of reality, as we saw and practised in the first chapter of this book – it is there, all around us and when approached with an attentive and respectful mind, it can be revealed. It can inspire curiosity, awe, insight. But the liveliness of creative discovery requires something beyond the gaze, even the ethnographic gaze: it needs childishness. Not in the sense of immaturity, silliness and infantile behaviour, but in the sense of Handke's poem and Wenders' opening scenes: of what William Blake called innocence.

To see a world in a grain of sand
And a heaven in a wild flower,
Hold infinity in the palm of your hand
And eternity in an hour. (Blake, 2013, p. 649)

The imaginoscope, if applied to the feelings, can help us to do just that. Let's do an experiment. If you live in an apartment block, consider the building you live in and which is part of your inmost everyday existence. If not, think instead of the building where your workplace is located or where you spend much of your time studying. Which parts of it do you really know? Which do you rarely visit or perhaps have never even seen? Take time to explore this apparently well-known building. If physically possible, take the elevator up to the top floor (if that is not the floor you use every day) or down to the cellar. Use an entrance you normally do not take. If your building has a staircase and you never use it, do so now. Take your time, advance slowly and carefully, take in everything you normally do not notice. That is what you would do – what you probably did – when you were a child. You would explore the attics, the little used wardrobe, the dark subterranean corridors, you would try the handles of doors that were probably locked but sometimes led to something really fascinating: a technician's cabinet, an unused dead-end room, an abandoned cellar box. Find that kind of space now. Look, smell, breathe. You could tell an ethnographic story about it, like we did in Chapter 1. This time, however, let's do something different. Think of Narnia, think of the Secret Garden. Tell yourself a fairy tale of your discovery. There was a grown-up person who lived/ worked in a building which s/he knew very well. Once s/he got lost and...

In order to be childish in this sense, you do not have to be a child physically. According to philosopher Gaston Bachelard (1969b, p. 114) *'childhood is the well of being'*. One can draw from it at any point in life. The series of childhood stories about little Nicolas by René Goscinny and Jean-Jacques Sempé (2020) is written by adults primarily for children, but also for the authors themselves and for other adults. It stems from the 1960s but it has a huge and – it seems – unending readership in all age categories. In fact, the audience reading and identifying with the heroes of the stories is expanding: originally they were rather aimed at boys but currently women and girls are as much *'les copins'* as the male readership. Nicolas is a child recounting his everyday life with his buddies from school. Everything is an adventure for the kids and everything inspires humour, interest, eagerness, an intensity of feelings: a heap of sand in the school yard, a gift of coloured pencils from grandma, a downpour of rain, a cousin getting married. Nicolas is an ordinary kid: he loves sweets, he likes football, he likes having fun. He is not a very good pupil, but neither is he a bad one. He dreams of being an aviator. He does not stand out in the stories nor in the drawings accompanying the stories. He is each of us, readers, and he is, of course, the authors of the stories and the drawings. Telling tales of childhood, on the terms of the child, in a child's language and imagery, brings out the childishness in us. It lends voice to the inner child to look at and narrate the world around her. But there is more to the childish perspective than this – there is also an interpretation of the world that very strongly uses and invites the creative spirit. The best genre for expressing this mode of understanding is the fairy tale.

The role of fairy tales as educational tools and catalyzers of discovering of self and others has been extorted by many authors, among them Bruno Bettelheim who, in his *Uses of Enchantment* (1976), proposes a psychoanalytic reading of popular fairy tales. He argues that fairy tales help children to deal with major psychological issues such as oedipal conflict, and to deal with anger and violent emotions without giving in to them. Fairy tales offer plots of both improbable hope and darkest fears, which are usually absent in educational narratives. They thus serve an important psychotherapeutic aim. In Pierre Péju's (1981) reading, fairy tales are more than that: they play a philosophically enlightening role. Péju does not agree that they can be reduced to psychoanalytic formula and upholds, instead, a poetics of the fairy tale which cannot and should not be forced into a simplified functional interpretation. The tale has a voice of its own and by listening to its rhythms and respecting the enchantment it brings, we can learn about the ambiguous and irreducible that we all encounter but which children are more sensitive towards than adults. We can all – children as well as grown-ups – immerse ourselves in such stories and follow the narrative currents.

> To know how to tell fairy tales makes it possible to realize momentarily such a 'becoming a child again'. The illuminated features of a storyteller, the open mouth, suspended finger; the face encloses narrator, listener or reader, the time of a story. (p. 71)

Then spaces and connections appear that are not possible to discern in more realistic and adult tales. They awaken the mythical consciousness without invoking the supernatural or sacred. The narrator should let her- or himself be carried by the story, for the sake of itself, irrespective of any end or project. Besides, and importantly, they bring back the childhood that has become marginalized through socialization into the consciousness and experiential ability of the adult person. This is the ability that Gaston Bachelard (1969b) calls *les noyaux d'enfance*, the kernels of childhood: the energies that provide the power of metamorphosis.

Fairy tales can also help the ethnographer to maintain a reflective stance in the field, embracing the poetics and the ambiguities and allowing herself to be propelled in unexpected directions, organization theorist Anna Zueva (2021) argues in an essay dedicated to the uses of fairy tales in ethnographic research. It is a genre that allows the observer to be open minded towards complexity and contradiction: the king is both noble and proud, the granny is both wise and actually a witch. The moral is not always obvious and, the more interpretive space is allowed to the features of the genre, the less the reading is forced into simplifying evaluations and categories, the more it invites wonder. The fairy tale allows us to see – it is not necessarily an escapist pastime – without robbing the world of mystery. It makes it possible to keep the child's intensity of experience from falling prey to feeding self-indulgence or self-interest. Using fairy tales to read the observed world makes it possible to let other voices speak through us, not even necessarily personalized or connected with specific identities. It is an 'archetypal sensemaking narrative' (ibid., p. 156), a multi-dimensional and unruly device that makes sure that stories do not revolve solely around the narrator or the points she wishes to make. It embraces liminality and takes into account unclear, conflicting feelings and phenomena. It gives food for reflection, and cherishes unfamiliarity.

Last but not least, fairy tales offer a kind of closure that is not necessarily wrapped up in a conclusion. When photographer Kirsty Mitchell's mother, Maureen, died, she was overcome with grief. She was missing her mother profoundly, thinking of how she always had a book near her, how they used to read fairy tales together when Kirsty was little. One day, sitting at her kitchen table, Kirsty started to draw. Out of the drawing came a 5-year long artistic journey, the result of which – *Wonderland* – I saw at an exhibition at Stockholm's Fotografiska museum (Mitchell, 2018). The project is a photographic fairy tale, consisting of 74 pictures. In the words of curator Lisa Hydén,

> The exhibition is a true fairy tale experience – like a brightly colored firework display where magic and reality meet on the journey we call life. (Mitchell, 2018)

Kirsty set out into the forests surrounding her home in the English countryside to take pictures of scenes that resonated with her memories of the fairy tales she used to love so much as a child. She depicted models made up and dressed as fairy-tale characters, posing against the woodland scenes. There is no real plot and the images do not illustrate any actual tales: it was led by the artist's feelings and has a dreamlike quality, rather than a strictly narrative structure. Mitchell had no team of assistants working with her and the whole project was created by herself with the help of a few friends, all entirely self-funded. It was allowed to unravel, unfold, from a relationship between her grief, the fairy-tale aura, the surrounding nature and an active, acutely felt inspiration she was following. The main character, expressing the ebbs and flows of this journey, is depicted encountering various settings, scenes and other magical characters. She slowly wanders between alluring springs, enchanted summers, magical autumns, drawn towards a vastness of winter. The last photo depicts her walking towards a small cottage embraced by a winter landscape. It is the only photo where she is turned away from the viewer, and it is entitled 'Home'. I saw the exhibition in a wintertime Stockholm. The museum building was embedded in a steep hill silver-plated by frost. I was still mourning my mother, Krystyna, who had died over a decade ago. She also loved books and I have many memories from childhood, of shared experiences of reading fairy tales with her. I was immediately drawn into the exhibition, at first I walked through it impulsively and fast, stopping longer only at some of the images that I connected with strongly. Then I returned to the beginning and followed, this time very slowly, each picture in sequence, like one would with the Way of the Cross in a Catholic church: step by step, ebb and flow, until the last image, 'Home'. And just like Mitchell, I found consolation.

Here are some guidelines of how to use the imaginoscope to lend mythical voice to your inner child.

- Think of a fairy tale you liked particularly when you were little. Try to bring back the feelings and images that held you enthralled back then. If you have access to the original text or film, watch or read it again and try to disconnect your adult persona.
- Consider the main character in the fairy tale: who are they? What are they like? Imagine yourself entering the tale. You can borrow the part of one of the characters or invent your own. Who are you? What do you look like? What do you do?
- You probably have a plushie toy or a doll, even though you now are a grown up. If not, buy one. What is her or his name? Touch it gently. Invite it for a stroll in the park (you can keep it hidden in your pocket or backpack but please think of it while you walk, try to talk with it as if you were a child again).

4.2. Practice: Pursuing enchantment

Fairy tales are a powerful source of archetypes. Psychologists, philosophers and artists reach for them for inspiration and to understand the human condition. Inventing your own ending to a childhood story can be an act that mobilizes the energy needed to find solace, forgiveness, or a new beginning (transformation). I propose to work with a fairy tale that is probably known to all of us: Cinderella. Replace the traditional ending with your own personal one; don't be influenced by how it 'should' end, invent your own. Please sketch your ending in the form of a brief narrative or a haiku.

The responses to this challenge were different from the former ones: while the others were quite different from each other, these tended to follow one of a few themes. I will narrate the themes here with one or two examples of how they usually worked. Many of the short stories were deeply personal and I shall, of course, not break the confidence of their authors by repeating them here.

The first and most popular theme is epic and depicts the emancipation of Cinderella. She realizes that she does not need a prince or, indeed, an inaccessible father.

After the ball, Cinderella's life changed completely. The girl realized that she had the right to be independent and make her own decisions. She decided to move away from the stepmother and her pesky sisters, and because she was very hardworking, she found a job with a friendly craftsman and, with time, advanced to master cratfswoman and then, partner and co-owner. (Justyna)

In some stories the prince, also, is emancipated.

The prince found Cinderella thanks to the lost shoe. They got married but they were not happy – Cinderella could not get used to the royal palace, she felt uncomfortable. So they both packed their things and moved to another city where they made a living as shoe traders. Their shop became immensely popular. Because the whole world knew about their family history with shoes! (Yana)

Sometimes the ending is not an ending, but a beginning:

Cinderella ran out of the castle and started to rush home. After some time, she realized that she was only wearing one shoe, which slowed her down considerably. So she took off her shoe and threw it into the field. She continued to run barefoot. A thought occurred to her: she had never felt so free! She had just come out of the ball, to which she went of her own free will, and now, throwing her slipper away, she also rejected the possibility of spending the rest of her life with the prince. She realised that she was not even sorry. Getting to know the prince was a confirmation that if she wanted something, she could achieve something, but she did not want to become his wife and live in the palace. That was not her dream. Running around like this and thinking about her life, Cinderella came up with a new plan.

She ran lightning fast into the house. She looked around – her stepmother and sisters were not there yet. As fast as she could she packed her things and set off on a journey ahead. Free and independent. What will happen to her now? We don't know, from now on Cinderella is writing her own fairy tale...(Karolina)

The second plotline is romantic: the prince and Cinderella find each other. But, unlike in the tale, they do not need all the superficial trappings: the shoe, the recognition game. But they do need something to be able to recognize each other. In Joanna's story, it is a garden.

The next morning, after the ball, Cinderella woke up on a bench in the royal gardens. She had lost one shoe, and didn't quite remember what had happened – too much alcohol, apparently. She heard someone approaching and, embarrassed, she hid in the nearby bushes. She saw gardening tools lying about and decided to take them and to play the role of a gardener so as not to be noticed. But she was improvising really well and caught the attention of the master gardener. He loved what he saw and praised her good work. Cinderella decided to stay on, as, frankly, she did not feel very much like returning home to her dysfunctional family. Months passed and the prince started to carefully observe the garden, and was falling in love with it. The garden bloomed and expanded like never before, it was almost magical. The prince spent more and more time in the garden. One day he caught the sight of the new apprentice gardener and then he knew it all: he had finally met his soul mate and was able to connect with her forever. (Joanna)

Ania's story is more traditional, but here the prince does not need any signs at all: he has seen her face.

Cinderella runs out of the ball at midnight, losing her slipper at the same time. The prince tries to catch up with her, but to no avail. On one of the steps, I find a small, beautiful shoe, but he does not need it for anything because he remembers his beloved's face very well, but he wants to return it to her personally. The day after the ball, he calls the best painter from all over the kingdom. The prince carefully describes the appearance of his beloved. The artist manages to recreate the beauty of an unknown girl. The prince sets off on a journey with the portrait to all the brides who were invited to the ball. One of the last houses was that of Cinderella's stepmother. The stepmother, with her daughters, tries to lock Cinderella in the basement, but thanks to the strength and cunning of the girl, she manages to escape. Just as she leaves the cellar, the prince's carriage arrives. The one who looks at the girl immediately recognizes her as his beloved. Despite her stepmother's objections, the prince manages to persuade Cinderella to become his wife, gives her back her lost slipper as well as the portrait. He takes her to the castle, where they get married and live happily ever after. The End. (Ania)

A few tales revealed other romantic happy endings:

After a long and complicated search, the prince finally finds Cinderella. However, she rejects his proposition: after all she does not know him that well. But his sister, the princess, is accompanying him in his search and the two women meet each other and fall in love. And they live happily ever after. As you can see, love comes as a surprise. (Anna)

The third theme is tragic: love is absent. Often it is the prince who is not serious, and Cinderella remains unloved.

first chime of the clock:
girl runs away from a lover
second chime of the clock:
prince runs after stranger
third chime of the clock:
he finds another girl (who cares about shoes?)

poor orphan
still pealing peas
and loneliness (Aneta)

Sometimes the whole story is just out of joint.

Cinderella ran out of the ball because the clock in the castle tower had already struck midnight. The prince, enchanted with Cinderella, followed her in front of the castle, but not seeing her on the horizon, he returned to the ball. It is true that he got contact information on Cinderella's social media (because now everything is happening there), but he did not make an attempt to contact...the day after the ball, two, three...silence...this is how the story of the meeting of these two ended. (Martyna)

The tragic ending may be due, however, rather to foolishness than malice or wickedness:

Foolish prince!
looking for shoe, not a face
such silly ambition (Maria)

The fourth theme is, again, tragic, but it is not only love that is lost, it is magic itself.

Such disappointment:
I do not lose my shoes but
my magical sheen. (Angelika)

Finally, there were also a few more ambivalent, indefinite endings, like this lovely and puzzling haiku:

Eternity with you all, with
a slipper lost
is magic to me. (Kasia)

The haiku form enables the writer to express feelings of indefiniteness and longing:

Cherry trees blossom

in rays of the sun,
alas, you do not (Chris)

Finding your own ending to a popular fairy tale is one way of working with the genre. Another is to invent a fairy tale all of one's own. Consider the following challenge:

May 2020, another week of pandemic isolation...It's a strange and difficult time. You have become used to some things, but others are becoming more and more unbearable. Daily rituals help you to cope with the feeling of uncertainty and increasing chaos. You thought that nothing much can surprise you anymore. And yet...One morning, while you were eating your breakfast, a potted flower standing on your windowsill spoke up and said...

The responses of my students to this task were very diverse and it is difficult to find common threads or themes. However, the flower usually spoke words of wisdom. In Joanna's story he made her pause and be present.

'Imagine Joanna, what you would be doing at this point if there were no pandemic.' Of course, I thought it would be Tuesday, I would be moving between the office and the university in my favourite skirt. I would probably arrange a beer party in the evening, and at the back of my head I would have a thought that I need to pack, because I am going to Warsaw over the weekend. I would be thinking about having to buy train tickets, perhaps on the iphone.

The flower spoke again and asked, 'Do you think you'd have a better mood than you are now?' I answered: I think so, yes. But for some time after the conversation I had with my flower, I have been trying not to think about what would be, but what is and what can be. I don't anticipate so much. I think that the pandemic allowed for a momentary 'freeze-frame', to think about the here and now. (Joanna)

Sometimes the flower provoked someone to reflect on what they really want.

And who would have thought such a time would come
When in the comfort of your own four walls
We'll start dreaming such simple dreams
Like wanting to look at the clouds again.

After these words, there was silence...I wondered if it was still a dream or if I had gone completely crazy being in isolation for several months. Immersed in a state of increasing uncertainty, I realized that I was slowly losing my inner peace, that the only thought in my head was 'just to survive'.

'Enough of this stagnation!' I screamed in my thoughts. 'I want to enjoy life again, I want to feel the meaning of being alive again...' (Natalia)

But that does not mean 'going back to normal'. Indeed, several stories question the 'normalcy' of reality before the pandemic. Marianna's story ends on a sobering note, when, after a brief celebration of inter-species solidarity, the flower realizes that

when everything is back to normal, your rat race will start all over again – the eternal climbing the career ladder, the pursuit of promotion, titles, money...You will step into the avalanche of consumerism yet again. Breakfast will be skipped again and you will do things on the go, on the way to somewhere, to your so-called 'normal'. (Marianna)

The plant would offer words of warning. It was, after all, not just a plant, but Mother Nature's child.

'Is it time to wake up?'

I froze, mug suspended in the air, halfway to my mouth. I knew right away that what was happening was real and I wasn't dreaming or hallucinating, so I replied.

'From what?'

And then something even weirder happened, the plant bowed one of the stalks towards me, as if expecting me to catch it. As soon as I did that, I moved to another world, full of the most beautiful vegetation and the richest fauna I have ever seen in nature. The sky above me had shades of pink and purple, and even though it was the middle of the day, I could clearly see the constellations of stars.

'Where are we?' I asked.

'In Paradise', she replied. 'Cataclysms begin to happen on the Earth you know. This is how Nature deals with over-exploitation. Soon everything will be destroyed or the planet will be reborn. For this to happen, we need to wake up and see what is really important.'

'It's so beautiful here...will people really destroy the Earth? Can they save the planet? Why are you telling me all this?'

'Because you know how to appreciate beauty. People will be given a chance so they can learn to live in harmony with Mother Nature. My and your mother loves us and you and cannot just write us all off.' (Małgorzata)

But sometimes it just offered simple yet profound words of comfort.

If someone forced me to get up in the morning, apply make-up and take the tram to the university, often checking something 'important' on my phone or reading a book, I would not be able to do it. But you are now doing things that are my daily life: you often sit by the window, looking out, wondering, you drink a lot of water and look almost like a flower –you are beautiful without make-up...you cope well in the conditions of plant life – respect to you, you are a strong being.

    P.S. I will talk to my flowers myself soon now (Yuliia Savytska)

Natalia confessed that the challenge brought her much joy and made her turn to her potted flowers with love and care. The story is a result of that.

I'm glad you're here. We are fine together. I hope you will feel much better today than you did recently! You know, I'm actually happy about our trip to the countryside. All in all, you have always complained that you are missing the best moments of spring that you spend on the run in Kraków, and now you have the opportunity to lie in the grass and feel flower petals falling on you from the fading cherries. So much good of this whole situation that this year you will make strawberries straight from the plot before they are over! Somehow the air does me good. See for yourself – a new green shot! We are good together. I'm glad you're here. (Natalia)

In some of the stories it was the flower that craved attention. A relationship is beginning to form...

'You enjoy your breakfast, yes? And when will you feed me, hmm? I haven't gotten any water since yesterday, and I've been given fertilizer some two weeks ago. You are extremely irresponsible. I'm dying here, you know?' I looked at the flower with compassion. But truth to be told, it's a terrible drama queen: I water it diligently, and he still manages to put off a show with falling leaves and fading flowers. I

looked back at the oatmeal bowl and said in a calm voice:
'Maurycy,' that's the name of the flower, 'do not dramatize.
I'll water you in a moment, no worry. And I can't give you
fertilizer more than once a week, because you'll get sick.'

'I don't dramatize, I don't dramatize!' Maurycy exclaimed
in a dramatic tone, 'If I die, you will have a bigtime existential
crisis, you'll see! You sit at home all day and you can't even
take care of your flowers!'

I sighed and got up to water Maurice. After all, I am not
afraid of existential crises, I have already found my purpose
in life. It is keeping Maurice and all his merry family alive,
which is systematically increasing since the pandemic began.
Nihil novi, ladies and gentlemen, nihil novi...(Anna Żur)

The flower would, at times, reach out to its human friend to
make him realize that the relationship has always been there,
waiting to develop.

'I've been standing on this windowsill for so many years, we
haven't had a chance to talk yet. The life of a young human
is probably too fast.'

That's true, flower, we never talk,' I replied.

'Well, isn't this the best possible moment to slow down a
bit? Look deeper into yourself? Talk to an old potted friend?'

'Yeah, you're right. The moment has come, let's use it
properly,' I said. (Arkadiusz)

Plants are compassionate, but so are humans.

'Kasia, you humans are really brave. If someone took away
the palm next to me, my favourite pot, or stopped watering
me... I wouldn't survive. But you do. No friends, favourite
restaurants closed, no family...You humans cry sometimes,
but you also laugh. You just go on living and you do so well.

I admire you.'

    I answered:

    'Monstera...you don't realize how good you are at surviving! I didn't buy you in a flower shop, or the nearby store. I found you all dried out, without water and without a pot. You were lying about in the chute at the bottom of our block. But in a few days you sprung alive...because you wanted to live, you overcame it all. With my help, you made it. You were strong. We're all strong together if that's what we want.' (Kasia)

The plant would sometimes speak up to inform of its own feelings. One of Aleksandra's flowers revealed to her that:

If I could move
I would reach out with an awkward arm
to that orchid standing on the shelf
and soften the whiteness of her velvets. (Aleksandra)

The conversation with the flower opened eyes towards the wider world.

'Good that it's almost summer. I was already fed up with this artificial heat from the radiators. The dry air was bad for my leaves. And now...Whoa, holy Chlorophyll Mother! Now it's fairy tale time!' he said, turning the leaves towards the sun's rays, which shamelessly burst into the room.

    Hearing that, I looked up uncertainly. First on the ficus standing on the windowsill, and then on the window. I didn't know what surprised me more. The fact that the ficus talks to me or that it's actually summer. (Weronika)

In haiku form the message could be quite powerful.

For the second month I don't see planes landing.
This strange new reality.
It's good that the Sun and the Moon did not leave their sentry.
(Anna)

New connections become visible.

you finally have time
be amazed as you need to
everyone longs so much (Paulina)

Natalia's flower was a veritable potted Pythia.

Spring, blooming
You, alone
I, withering

The world is waning
Joy flees too quickly
I'm waiting for better tomorrow (Natalia)

The flower is calm and observant:

Birds outside the window
Travel throughout the skies.
Ordinary life. (Kinga)

Agnieszka's flower not only spoke to her, but gave her a gift –
something it knew she would appreciate from now on:

Good morning Agnieszka! I have clothed my thoughts in three
lines of poetry to give you some respite. I know how you enjoy
words. Don't forget that life goes on all the time...
the forest is calling you today

serenity and peace live there
life does not vanish (Agnieszka)

And, finally, it offered Karolina the words of true inter-species compassion:

Like me, you watch spring
From behind the window.
Longing. (Karolina)

The first imaginoscopic challenge was about an existing fairy tale, one which everyone probably had known in their childhood. The authors merged their own feelings with the enchantment of the well-known plot and turned it narratively in a direction of their own creation. In the second they used enchantment to tell a fairy tale of their own making. Both types of narrative arrived at a poetic moment where the authors realized something about themselves and their situation at the time they spun the tale. But the moment was only a narrative device and the story unravelled towards an ending or a coda that was, again, aligned with their own feelings, even if on a different level. That is – all but the more puzzling haikus I quoted last in this chapter.

5. Collection: Catching the poetic moment

5.1. The poetics

The imaginoscope can be applied to the soul, on the farther side of the Imagination. It helps to grasp the enchantment and hold it for a longer time, offers a way of perceiving that is, in itself, haiku-like: a poetic epiphany. The word derives from the Greek term *epiphaneia* which means materialization of something divine, a manifestation. Social sciences use the term in order to refer to particular moments of insight marking a creative breakthrough and inviting acts of imagination. Ad van Interson, Stewart Clegg and Arne Carlsen (2017) argue that such moments are not privatized experiences uniquely reserved for individual geniuses but are relational – they take place within processes of experience and exchange. They are usually far from the stereotypical strikes of lightning from nowhere, but can be invited by inquiry, persistent trials and tribulations.

They emerge in the form of feelings from practice which is often collective and they can be shared with others in the form of communicable ideas. Epiphanies can be found in small, everyday things and can be both pleasant and unpleasant. They require an openness and knowledgeability that enable one to grasp serendipity when it occurs. In fact, epiphany 'befalls', but usually just the persistent, as a result of an intense multi-sensuous involvement. And they often come betwixt and between what is structured and better known, in liminal time. What they lead to is more of a mystery: epiphanies are open-ended and make it possible to transcend linear understandings (Weick, 2006). This is where the imaginoscope comes in useful: to collect them and turn them into meaningful patterns.

What interests us in our quest are the instances when epiphanic moments lead into a more lasting sense of wonder and open-endedness – what organization theorist Heather Höpfl (1995) calls poetics, a narrative mode in which 'the meaning is always ambivalent and resonates with the flux of experience' (p. 176). It embraces and cherishes ambiguity, creates resonances for what is not fully defined, even impossible to express. While rhetorical narratives strive to suppress ambiguity and direct towards a linear and fixed course, the poetical mode opens new perspectives, bursts out of categories, allows us to look under the surface. Poetics is a spontaneous cultural force that helps to embrace ambiguity and ambivalence and to seek inspiration, and cannot be managed or caught. But it can be found – as a result of an epiphanic moment focused on ambivalence and inspiration.

Philosopher of the imagination, Gaston Bachelard (1969a), speaks of the poetics of space. The imagination: dreams and reverie, unravels in a space beyond the external, material. It does not suppress it or replace it, but it unravels under the surface of the perceived reality. So, for example, a house is a house of bricks and mortar – but not just that.

Through poems, perhaps more than through recollections, we touch the ultimate poetic depth of the space of the house (p. 6).

The external space simplifies and makes this inner, poetic space look like something secondary, perhaps a reflection of reality that exists only in our mind. But once we are ready to leave the material for the imaginary, we may realize that the spaces mingle and fuse and we, human beings, are entangled in them.

Outside and inside are both intimate – they are always ready to be reversed, to exchange their hostility. If there exists a border-line surface between such an inside and outside, this surface is painful on both sides. (p. 217-18).

Bachelard proposes that we need to listen to poets in order to be able to make this realization, following the flow of 'waves of newness...over the surface of being' (p. 222). The role of language is, in rhetorical speech, to define, to enclose through the ascription of meaning. Through poetic expression it opens up to the world of imagination which 'gravitates about a value' (1969a, p. 171). Its reality is immaterial but profoundly human, an elemental power, and 'must be lived in their poetic immensity' (ibid., p. 201). In this space images and events appear not by the law of causality which we are used to from the material space, but by the law of attraction and association that occurs between the mind and the images, between the images themselves. The dream has a narrative order but it is not linear, causal or rhetorical. Sometimes it is too difficult to narrate, even if we remember the dream we had during the night quite vividly. But ordinary language narrative logic often fails to grasp it. Instead, it unfolds in poetic rhythms, invoked by attention. If we apply attention to the imagined or dreamed image, the words seem to come by their own power. However, if we focus too much, they may disappear.

Dream and reverie are not tools but something like transportation vehicles, carrying the person in what Bachelard calls 'space of *elsewhere'* (ibid., p. 184): which is everywhere but with the added depth of imagination. Everything touched by attention in this extended reality 'can be the seed of a world, the seed of a universe imagined out of a poet's reverie' (Bachelard, 1969b: 1). And this is where poetic language and spatiality concur. These spatial seeds also have an existence as symbols, which are the stuff that both sensemaking and communication are made of. The imaginoscope can be placed in this vital intersection between the experienced and the expressed, and used to produce a pattern which does not petrify reality into a definition or rhetorical statement.

Here it how it works. Think of the last dream you can remember. Concentrate intensely on the images and let them unfold in your mind, even if not linked by any specific plot or order. Try to see them as fully and vividly as you can. What colour are they? How do they move? Are there any sounds in your dream? Any smells, experiences of taste? What embodied feelings do they invoke in you? Focus as much as possible. Now try to write down your dream. It can be a story, a few sentences or a poem. I write poetry and many of my poems originate in dreams. And not only the poems – much of my writing, including this book, is more or less directly inspired by my dreams.

Even if the poetic mode is not the dominant way of writing in our times, it is a potentially viable way of artistic and scientific expression. Social scientists Jenny Helin, Matilda Dahl and Pierre Guillet de Monthoux (2020), invoking Bachelard's phenomenology of dreaming, propose steps to the creation of generative moments for and between authors wishing to write poetically. First of all, they endorse the importance of space, or the creation of a new spatiotemporality to reconnect to the moment, the place, themselves and each other. To explore the possibilities this brings, they set out into the Swedish countryside in a caravan, inviting their interlocutors – farmers, whom they were studying ethnographically. This enabled them to go to their premises but stay in a separate space. They explored and observed, but had a room of their own, to which they invited their interviewees for a chat and a coffee and where they later could talk about their impressions and write. The caravan made it possible for them to awaken what Bachelard (2013) refers to as the verticality of time. Horizontal time unfolds in a linear way: from the past towards the future. It lacks depth and is perceived as something external to the human being. In contrast, vertical time happens when we consider the moment, which is the only real time that can be experienced, and is suspended between two voids (the past which does not exist anymore and the future that does not exist yet). It is not continuous but disruptive and immersive: it has height and depth and one can plunge into it. Once accessed, vertical time is experienced as multi-dimensional, complex and difficult (if not impossible) to measure. It is the time of becoming and of simultaneities, not just of one's own experience but potentially also with others. Bachelard speaks of an 'androgynous instant' (p. 59) uniting the masculine vigour and feminine gentleness. This is the instant where opposites meet and create a synthesis which is – makes us – alive. The caravan created, for Helin and her colleagues (2020), a point of access to vertical time while being in the field, doing ethnography and writing it down. It gave them a space to think, talk and engage with the world without the horizontal line, unfolding and ordering chronologically words, thought and rhythm. Not unexpectedly, they did part of their writing in the form of poetry: in the field notes and later, in the written reports from their research. They speak of their caravan as their seashell which gave them a peace from the ordinary noise that disrupts poetic rhythms of life. From within its sheltered space they invited a different, non-horizontal attention. They could focus on reverie and conversation, on the slow rhythms of thinking and sharpening their senses through sensitivity. They describe their caravan as a kind of 'pause mechanism'. In a similar vein, together with a co-author (Kociatkiewicz and Kostera, 2015), we depict the spatial construction of the labyrinth as a device that is slowing us down, represents the transitional and unmanaged, lets us pursue multiple meanings and ends. Both the caravan and the labyrinth help to escape linearity and reclaim the meandering, living language. They provide a shelter for the poetic moment.

To recuperate: on order to switch from the rhetorical, linear mode of being and expression to the poetic, we need to enter unto poetic moment and hold on to it, renouncing the horizontal perception of time and entering vertical time. To do that we need some kind of shelter. I can be a house, a caravan or a labyrinth but do not have to be exactly either of those. It can be any other kind of shelter that makes us feel ontologically safe – to experience a sense of basic trust and be able to experience whatever is coming our way. And, at the same time, the shelter must slow us down fundamentally, snatch us out of the pace of everyday life. It can be a garden, a favourite calm place in a library, a quiet café, even a silent spot in our workplace, where there is no commotion, no disruption, nothing threatening to seize our attention. Like in the practice with observation in Chapter 1, we need to become intensely focused on everything around us – and, at the same time, on everything inside us. That is what the imaginoscope does in this instance. Catching the poetic moment means opening a doorway between the external space – and the internal. In other words, it is about enchantment.

American psychologist James Hillman (2017) speaks of the invisible dream underpinning human reality, which is as necessary as the air we breathe: without it space is dead, there is a sucking void designed as a morbid replacement for imagination that connects people. The 'goods' we surround ourselves with become mere 'stuff', 'deaf and dumb consumables' (p. 110), our knowledge becomes valueless, our communication loveless. Love together with imagination focuses on the Other; it is a kind of enchantment that yields closeness. Connection happens when there is an imaginative interest actively and intensely at work. Real connection with the Other and with the world requires mystery. For life is not just a natural process; it is a mystery. How we imagine it is as important as how we conceive of it rationally. Most immediately, it can be experienced as a sense of beauty. James Hillman (1989) regards beauty as intrinsic to the human soul, always accompanying it, it is a necessity, the meaning of and the key to mystery and enchantment that 'touch[es] our senses, reach[es] the heart and attract[s] us into life' (p. 302). Beauty is the revelation in the here and now, 'sheer appearance for its own sake' (p. 295), the way that things announce themselves and speak for themselves. The awakening of the soul is a process of beauty, and it is an appreciation of beauty. It is primordial and profoundly human: what drove our ancestors to the amazing cave paintings, what still makes us connect to nature, to the world. It is both spiritual and material – it is a process of manifestation, the moment of becoming which happens as a fusion of mind and matter. Poet and philosopher Franco Bifo Berardi (2018) believes that this moment can be found in the poetic rhythms of breathing.

Poetry is the excess which breaks the limit and escapes measure. The ambiguousness of poetical words, indeed, may be defined as semantic overinclusiveness...Excessiveness is the condition of revelation, of emancipation from established meaning and of the disclosure of an unseen horizon of signification: the possible (p.20).

To live poetically, *vivre poétiquement* (Morin, 2020, p. 261) is human – it means bringing (back) in the notion of the good life as central into our world. Poetic living can save us from losing our humanity, even in the darkest and bleakest of times. It can also help to save the planet, Edgar Morin argues in his book about the lessons we need to draw from the COVID-19 pandemic. We need to change the path, from the quantity and growth oriented one we have been following more and more obsessively for the last decades, to a slow one, concentrated on the quality of experiences and things. We have to begin to see more, appreciate the human condition, existence, life itself. If we do that we can awaken, even resurrect solidarities with others and with the localities and nature which we belong to. It is helpful to think of Gaston Bachelard's (1969a) advice about how to approach the poetic dimension of space: it is essential to be able to see as if for the first time, through astonishment, which requires proceeding by means of a positive naiveté. Here are some further ideas of how to access that space (based on Kostera and Średnicka, 2016).

- Find a space where you feel sheltered from external rhythms. Make yourself at home there. Visit every day, even for a few minutes and disconnect from everything that preoccupies you.
- Think: who is your favourite romantic hero? Who do you identify with? Try to read a poem about him or her from time to time, and symbolically remember him or her.
- Appreciate silence. Think about what you can't hear and you might.
- Buy a book of poetry and place it on your bedroom table. Read a poem every night before falling asleep.
- Become interested in history, the great and the small, local. Always try to get to know the history of the organization you are working with.
- When visiting a new city or country, always try to get to know it through the eyes of local poets. Find at least one

poet from the place you visit and read at least one of his or her poems.

- Look up at the sky. What story can you see in the clouds today?

5.2. Practice: To live poetically

What is beauty?

This is a personal question, addressed to you personally. It does not concern a definition, nor a common opinion, nor what others think and write about it, nor how they proclaim it, nor what makes us think and speak of good taste. It is not about what is fashionable, pretty, cute, what others like. It is about what you are in awe of, even if no one else feels it or understands it, even if you feel it cannot really be expressed in words. This is about what makes you feel that life is real and true. It can be something huge and momentous, or it can be a small thing, a moment, one tiny iota. It does not have to be your only visual vision of beauty – we have many of them. But it has to be something that is important to you now, here, in this place and time.

Of all the tasks I assigned to my students this year, this one turned out to be the most popular among them, as well as the most creative. There were not two answers which were alike, and everyone had something important to say. All were personal, but some profoundly so – and these I shall not quote here. It is very difficult to find common threads, but I shall try to illustrate some of the flowing ideas that can be helpful to you, Readers, in your quest for beauty with the imaginoscope.

Beauty is, for many, art. Not necessarily great and public art – often it is the personal and relational. For example, Karolina found an old family photograph.

This old black and white: the photograph is beauty because it keeps memories on paper. The people depicted in it are beautiful for me. It's a pity that photos are being developed on paper more and more rarely these days, everything has gone digital. The paper photo: fragile, frayed at the edges – is an amazing moment passed on across time. I believe that this photo is real art. (Karolina)

Some chose film.

For me, the art of old films with Buster Keaton is beauty. Every time I watch movies in which he appears (even though I have seen them countless times), I am always overwhelmed by an amazing feeling of belonging despite complete difference. Different times, different means of expression. And yet...I love film and watch many different genres. I am often moved and inspired by them, but nothing works like Keaton. It is not only his physiognomy with his characteristic eyes and lack of a smile, but also some incredible energy that radiates from him off the screen. That's when I have the impression that I associate with something that is beauty. (Natalia)

Documentaries can also carry experiences of beauty.

I think of Mekas's film As I Was Moving Ahead Occasionally I Saw Brief Glimpses of Beauty, which I watched quite some time ago. It changed my perception of beauty and will probably stay with me forever. From that moment, I began to register beauty in seemingly trivial, everyday situations, the facial expressions of the people around me and their reactions...It is beautiful for me how in the era of the pandemic we (paradoxically) contradict the common view that humans cannot cope with freedom and that work takes up 3/4 of our life and that it determines the meaning of existence and happiness. The beautiful thing is that we are able to stop now, like the film shows, notice other people and devote time to them instead of working all the time – which is a bottomless well...(Maria)

Actors are able to express beauty when they do something unique.

For me, the definition of beauty is what is unusual, maybe even perplexing. Tilda Swinton is able to express this. (Szymon)

Several people talk about galleries and museums and of spending intimate time with works of art.

I love visiting museums but not as part of a guided tour. I like looking in my own pace. Sometimes I just stand and stare. This makes me happy, but not in any obvious way, it's more like an obstinate child than a sophisticated art critic (Natalia)

Music is, for many, a strong experience of beauty.

Beauty is about the moment and emotion...Live music moves me. I can close my eyes and hear, and feel, and breathe. (Karolina)

Beauty can be found in the details and in age.

For as long as I can remember, beauty, for me, was hidden in architecture. However, not in baroque churches or Art Nouveau palaces, but in dilapidated doors with a richly ornamented carved handle, huge wooden factory windows, staircases decorated with rosettes or tiles. Places like this always make me stop to see all the details. (Karolina)

Nature is beauty.

I will always associate beauty with the sea. It doesn't matter what country, what time of year it is, whether it's cold, rainy or sunny. Beauty is peace, unimaginable space. (Monika)

Not just the spectacular aspects of nature, but also life itself, and what is propitious for it.

Rain is beauty. It has not always been so for me. I used to dislike it and still, having a choice of rain or sun, I will choose sunshine. But to watch and listen to drops bouncing off the windowsill is good. Also because of climate change, of draught – I feel that nature rejoices when it rains. Beauty for me is something that brings life and creates balance in nature. (Olivia)

To take part in a regeneration of life is a special experience, despite the tragedy of the pandemic.

Beauty, especially during the pandemic, is the regeneration of our planet. A few days ago I was smoking a cigarette in front of my block, and a deer suddenly ran down my street. In the evening, I can see squirrels hiding under the cars. And during the day, returning from the store, I could observe a fox right in front of me, it was strolling, quite unimpressed, it [walked through] the parking lot. (Jakub)

Light is beauty.

For me, the essence of beauty has always been light, but not [that kind of] light, thanks to which I could better feel or understand a work of art, but light, which is, in itself, an independent and complete work of art. It helps life to take

on contrasts, mystery and spice in a special way. I mean both
the gentle rays of the sun that caress the tops of my feet in the
morning, the light sparkling in the snowflakes, and the rays
of warmth that the afternoon sun leaves in the apartments. I
see beauty mainly in the shape and dance of light, its shyness
and the boldness of entering our lives. (Aleksandra)

Being human is beautiful.

I am often amazed at the sight of another person. Not one
who looks as if he or she accidentally stepped into the
streets of Kraków right off a catwalk of New York Fashion
Week, but people who are unaware of their own beauty:
an older man who stands in front of me in a supermarket
line, a middle-aged woman who sits down, tired, in a seat
on the bus. They captivate me because their voices, despite
the lack of universalist ambitions, sound the most true and
fullest when they talk about what they have experienced. An
example of such beautiful, non-verbalised micronarrations
are the working hands immortalized by Henryk and Janina
Mierzecki[3]. This kind of beauty has always been important
for me, but even more so here and now, because it makes
me aware that we are all silent heroes of some great story, it
teaches patience, understanding and love for others. (Joanna)

Human beings at work, and especially those close to us, bring a
sense of profound beauty.

...the hands of my mother when she cooks, when she makes
dough. Her hands immersed in flour, when they carefully
knead the dough...(Olena)

Work itself is beauty.

For me, beauty is physical work, such as furniture renovation. The first strong feeling of beauty appears when I manage to peel off all the old, damaged layers: cracked varnish or an old stain, and somewhere there – finally – natural wood beginning to emerge: bright, clean, unblemished, almost like new. Once again I experience beauty when the work is finished and I can see the result of my work: different, but the same, with the same 'old' soul. (Zuzanna)

Imperfections are beautiful.

Beauty is the unique way our loved one looks at us and the sensitivity of human beings. Our imperfections are also beauty, as they make us unique and more human. (Roksana)

Katarzyna develops this idea further.

Recently I talked to my friend about who is beautiful and why, and we noticed that there is a great difference between pleasing, pretty, attractive – and beautiful. Beauty is an aspect of life, consciousness, knowing…Being pretty means having a pretty face, body, blemish-free, perfect, dreamlike. But being beautiful means having freckles, a clumsy nose, wrinkles, scars, marks, thinning hair. An aspect of being. Impossible to imitate, strange and fascinating. Beautiful means that not everyone likes it, but because it is not unlike everything else, breaking out of the pattern, evoking feeling…If someone calls me beautiful, then it would be because of my thoughts, because this someone sees me as something more than just schematic good looks. (Katarzyna)

Cities are beautiful, because they are human.

The city, waking up to life, is beautiful. I like to observe it from my window, there is something quite magical about it. I like to sit by the window for a few minutes in the morning, with a cup of tea, and watch. It is beautiful how the rays of the morning sun fall on the streets, how people are rushing to work, someone is riding a bicycle, and someone is running. The commotion of a morning, the city coming to life. (Ada)

The sense of belonging that beauty invokes is momentous.

But does beauty exist at all? Or is beauty everything, like God? I began to see it everywhere. Then I started asking myself, do I belong to this omnipresent beauty? I used to think of myself as not – beautiful. Now I think: if everything is beautiful, then I must be too?...Yes, life is beautiful. My friends are very beautiful, the place and the city where I live and where I come from. (Volha Kavalskaya)

Beauty dwells in everyday moments of attention.

For me, beauty is both aesthetically interesting and visually engaging. Beauty is something we can read in the eyes of another person. They express human emotions: positive, negative, different. Plants make me happy. Lilac, unfolding gently, and bold forget-me-nots. Ordinary human kindness and expressions of empathy are extremely beautiful and necessary. Sunsets, and clouds travelling across the sky. The smile of another. Dumplings, which I make with great care, are beautiful. (Magdalena)

It is a kind of relationship.

Beauty is a human experience that helps:
- in bad weather, to feel the smell of asphalt after rain,
- in an abstract image, to recognize something dear to your

heart.

- in a crazy art installation, looking like a pile of garbage, to see hidden deeper meaning,
- in a plant that turns towards the Sun, to recognize desire for life...(Yuliia Savytska)

Beauty is amazement, especially the beauty of others.

I am amazed by many things. To varying degrees, of course, but I see a lot of beauty in the world. If I were to name a few recent things, there is beauty in the ways that people try to stay close to each other, despite the self-isolation. The feeling of being together and keeping in touch, the night conversations, exchanging emotions, stories from the past or new ideas for baking a cake. But especially moments of understanding, when I come across something that shows how another person experiences the world. This is what makes life real. (Agnieszka)

Beauty is, finally, the mundane, even trivial, when taken into the heart.

...my teddy bear. It is not a work of art, but it is my first memory. And it is still with me. This little bear is always waiting for me in a warm and safe home. When I come back from a long journey or from my 'adult' life, he is there and shows that I always have a place to return to. This is the loveliest dimension of beauty one can imagine. Especially now. (Marta)

In Marta's tale, beauty creates a kind of solidity. But the ephemeral, too, is beautiful...

The light falling on the wall in my room...It makes me feel

warmth, goodness and meaning. Beauty is something that shows me that the world is still an undiscovered miracle. (Justyna)

The small things, so important.

Beauty is the scent of night-scented stock on a warm summer evening.
Reminiscence of the smile of a loved one who is no longer with us.
The dog's joy at your return, even when you were away for only 5 minutes.
All the tears that made us who we are. (Monika)

Beauty disrupts the linearity of time.

Recently, I was driving in my car and passing by tall, green trees. A few days ago: daisies growing in the yard, they formed a carpet. Today: my mother's laughter in our imperfect kitchen. Beauty is what makes me want to stop time. And it does. (Anna)

Beauty is my students.

The imaginoscope, which helps to define beauty as part of the life world, can be a powerful way to keep and preserve the poetic moment. However, even when expressed in a poetic form, it remains elusive and deeply personal, not really a tool for organizing. And that is as it should be: the role of epiphany is ultimately just that. In order to invite the poetic moment as a social actor, and take part in social life and organizing processes, it has to become manifest.

6. Bringing it back home: Art and organizing

6.1. Art as organizer

Art is work on the boundaries of the known reality, with the aim to explore the imagination and express the unexpressed and unexplored or little known. It is not about gaining replicable results or reliable knowledge, but, rather, about gaining an insight or an inspiration and sharing it with a public. It can be said to manifest and realize the poetic moment. When it is produced and displayed for public view (or published, recited, played), it becomes a social actor – or actant – in Bruno Latour's (2005) terminology: a non-human participant in social interactions, shaping and influencing relations. The imaginiscope can help us to make art enter public space, when we apply it to the hands and the whole human body. Now art makes a presence together with the transporter of the imaginoscope.

An example of such constant and keen presence is Stockholm School of Economics, one of the most respected business schools in the world. It offers a number of more or less educational programmes in business and management on all levels, from bachelor to PhD. It holds close contacts with the business community and takes pride in its practical orientation. What may come as a surprise to many unwitting visitors is that it actually looks like – and, in fact, is – an art gallery. By the main entrance to the monumental building in the city centre the guest encounters temporary installations that may upset the visitor's mind, drawing attention to contemporary problems such as migration and climate change. They are often visible and strong statements which inquire but offer no definite answers. Upon entrance the vast main hall presents an impressive permanent collection. For example, there is Maria Miesenberger's bronze statue, 'Leap of Faith', which speaks of courage, curiosity and determination, as well as posing questions about ambition, discipline and knowledge. Lars Arrhenius' video installation, 'Handels for Future!', is a playful yet also serious presentation of the school itself. What is it? For whom? What does it do for society? For the planet? The video is neither an advertisement, nor a brand building tool. It is at times optimistic and at times disturbing and it makes the viewer pause and reflect. The visitor can go for an art-finding quest in the vast building – there are works of art presented, or maybe hidden, in the corridors, such as the famous bronze sculpture 'Non-Violence' by Carl Fredrik Reuterswärd, representing a Colt Python .357 Magnum revolver with a knotted barrel. And upmost in the building, crowning the space of the library, the guest can find a massive permanent video installation by Lina Selander and Oscar Mangione, 'Soli Deo Gloria', an inquiry into history, memory and values. It presents connections between the history of business and social change and to spirituality.

SSE Art Initiative produces art exhibitions and symposiums addressed to the students, employees of the school, and to art-interested members of the public, in order to create knowledge at the intersection between economy and the arts. 'The aim is to create and encourage conversations, reflections and knowledge sharing,' says Tinni Ernsjöö Rappe from SSE Art Initiative (SSE Art Initiative, 2020). And it does. The school arranges meetings with the authors of the installations and experts connected to the questions raised by them. There are regular seminars and events on art-related topics, more or less directly connected with the exhibited artwork, as well as film screenings, poetry sessions and book circles inviting authors and performers. 'We hope the literature in the Literary Agenda opens up new worlds for students, helping them see circumstances from other people's perspectives. Future leaders will need this empathy and capacity for reflection,' says President Lars Strannegård (SSE Art Initiative, 2020). There are art talks around each individual artwork, primarily addressed to students, but with a possibility to attend (after registration) to the public. The website proclaims:

> Art has the capacity to provoke and inspire through artistic expression, communicating with our senses. It can enhance our potential for critical thinking and create a deeper understanding of ourselves and societal context. (ibid.)

There seems to be a genuine resonance between the artwork and the students. My own contacts with the school's community indicate that there is an ongoing social activity around the exhibits and a good participation in the events, such as the Dada Party organized close to Christmas in 2018 in one of the school's social spaces. There was music, spontaneous poetry, live performances, film and mulled wine. The attendance was good and diverse: the participants could not be limited to an age group, nationality or occupation. There were students, artists, academics, some children, and the atmosphere was that of a real carnival. I took the opportunity to inquire of some of the students and they ascertained me that the Art Initiative is one of the most cherished aspects of the studies. One of them said that the artwork made such a huge difference just by standing there, so even if it were never addressed in any way, things would, in his words, 'escalate'.

The artwork inhabiting the buildings of Stockholm School of Economics does much more than the usual passive decorating. It is placed strategically, so that it becomes involved in the everyday life of the school. It invites certain activities, such as searching, making connections, for example, between the advertisements for the school and the artwork about the school, both displayed in the entrance hall. They invade the mind because some of them are disturbing, and not at all pretty, such as the installation about climate change displaying turd-shaped weights symbolizing air pollution. They provoke discussions – and these discussions are supported by the formal structures of the school. The artwork is a social actor causing what the student called 'escalation'.

The spiritus movens behind the Art Initiative, organization theorist Pierre Guillet de Monthoux (1993) views art not just as an organizational actor but as a mode of management, which is, at its core, a 'journey in the aesthetic space' (p. 4) and the pursuit of what is possible. The current standard of business education is not only blind to this dimension, but strongly focused on one-sided utilitarianism. This does not make the artistic aspects go away but violates and banalizes them. Modern management is usually dull or ugly. It needs not be so, but a new sensitivity and language is needed to grasp and express this space.

We are not able to understand management without understanding art. It is impossible to understand economic development without an aesthetic perspective. (ibid., p. 1)

It can be claimed that, in order to understand this, we lack knowledge, and not just humanistic, but also purely economic. Pierre Guillet de Monthoux (1998) explains that modern economic thought was established as part of human and moral sciences. Social constructs, such as the market, organizing and management are all related to morality and aesthetics. The now dominant reductionist approach, presenting management as a purely technical and financial activity, is not rooted in the tradition of either practice or the historical body of knowledge. Rather, it appears this way because it has been hewn and simplified to fill an ideological function that has been made prominent under neoliberal capitalism. Another rupture that contributes to this loss of knowledge is the disconnection between economics on the one hand, and philosophy and the humanities on the other, which took place only a few decades ago. Pierre Guillet de Monthoux proposes to step back and take a look at the bigger picture, giving voice to some of the important classics, such as Adam Smith (1998) and Immanuel Kant (1993). The latter helps to understand art broadly, as a kind of practical moral compass that helps with ethical and moral questions. These sensitivities need to be integrated and not, as is common now, split off and presented as completely independent from managerial knowledge. But aesthetic knowledge cannot be purely theoretical. It is as important to include it into the day-to-day practices of organizations. Guillet de Monthoux (1998) situates it at the heart of interactions between the social and the technical aspects of organizing. It shows the way to new practices and meanings, and, by bringing in and embracing the bizarre and the unusual, it has the ability to navigate in highly uncertain contexts, deal with what seems to be irrationality, invite the paradoxical and strange into collective endeavours without destabilizing them, without opening them up to entropy and chaos. In other words, art is a social actor that is capable of bringing in inspiration and renewal derived from the untamed and unknown in a way that is relatively safe for social structures and processes. In Guillet de Monthoux's (1993) terms, it does that by virtue of the six abilities derived from the unity of management and art: to understand, to inspire, to liberate, to wonder, to intoxicate, to humanize, understand and wonder[4]. The ability to understand comes in the guise of taste and enables one to make decisions which are based on it. It offers a unique pathway to knowing – without concepts or notions. The person interacting with art can learn and gain insight from it without necessarily having to name or generalize. The capability of art to inspire means that art can invoke the mythical dimension, as especially the romantics were proficient at doing. Aesthetic symbols are made visible as a, or perhaps even the, truth. Art's potential to liberate consists of its mission to nurture and educate. It does not do so by fast results and effective techniques. Rather, it is a long process of gathering experience and showing alternative ways of reasoning. This is a democratizing ability. Wonder has been all but lost in modern societies. Art has the capacity to bring it back and make it central. But it can also teach how to admire without submission to any dogma. Intoxication, when achieved by the means of drugs and other chemical substances, can be dangerous for the health and difficult to consciously experience and control. Art is not a chemical substance, yet it has the literal ability to intoxicate, captivate, enthral. It mobilizes the imagination and liberates creative vision. To humanize means the ability to invite human beings and populate the aesthetic dimension. This way it keeps the aesthetic play alive and disalienates.

But that is not all. Art is also a keen organizer. Organization theorist Jean-Luc Moriceau (2018) argues that art actively participates in organizing processes: they provide performative expressions that serve as powerful communicators – of course, if invited by other participants. One interesting effect of this use of art is its problematizing potential. Art helps us to question the 'obvious' and taken for granted and it triggers affects that may help to interpret organizational phenomena. Art also readily becomes a facilitator in organizational learning processes. It helps to learn by ambiguity and ambivalence, it questions rather than offers ready answers and is really helpful in contexts marked by dynamism and uncertainty (Berthoin Antal, 2014). Ariane Berthoin Antal investigates artistic interventions in organizations and concludes that they invite multiple ways of knowing, and in particular embodied senses. They are also truly intercultural, providing opportunities to explore new ideas in the workplace and in everyday social settings in ways both imaginative and practical. Art helps to embrace a complexity perspective and is able to give a structure, perhaps even a narrative form, to multifaceted social processes (Letiche, 2000). In other words, art not only inspires a mindset that helps to face complexity, it can serve as an organizational actor buffering other actors and helping them to enter into complex dynamics.

Below are some guidelines of how to, with the help of the imaginoscope, take advantage of the presence of art in everyday social settings.

- Explore your neighbourhood and your workplace: are there any works of art displayed or hidden in the public or shared space that you have, or have not, noticed before? Get familiar with it, get to know its author. Look for additional information on the internet or in the local library.
- Find out if there currently exist tours or discussion groups focused on local artwork or architecture. If yes, consider joining. If not, organize one for your colleagues and friends.
- Think of the sculptures displayed in your city, village or

region. Which one is your favourite? Take time to visit it. Take pictures from different sides. What does it make you think and feel? Why is it your favourite? Make a post on social media open to the public about it. Try to convince others to visit it.

- Visit the local museum and look for artwork that seems to speak personally to you. Take a notebook with you. Write down your thoughts – what are these works of art saying to you?

- Visit the website of your local museum and try to learn about their permanent exhibitions. What is the relationship between the place/ region and the exhibited art? Can you find artwork with particularly strong ties? What do they make you feel and think?

6.2. Practice: To invite art

What work of art – it can be completely unrealistic, but it has to be something that really exists – would be displayed in the entrance hall to your workplace (school, university, city hall) in order to alter the value system for the better of the regular users of that space? Name the artwork and explain why you chose it. It can be a sculpture or visual art, something famous or less known, created by somebody else or yourself.

Here are some responses to this challenge from my students. Generally, they speak either of art accessible in the public domain or private art. If you are unfamiliar with some of the public artwork they mention, it may be interesting to check it on the internet (I strongly recommend this!). I will first present responses referring to the public and, later, to the private domain.

Some of the respondents chose different paintings by van Gogh. The students were well aware that the paintings were complex, even unsettling, but believed that was, indeed, the point. Art makes us aware of the big picture, in the words of

Anna, literally so.

I would exhibit Vincent van Gogh's painting 'Starry Night' in the main hall, because it gives me the impression that there is 'more to life' [than the mundane surroundings]. It's probably because of the colours and that the stars sit in a very dark sky. It makes me imagine that I am one of those stars, I look at the Earth and it seems so small, if at all visible: you can't see any people, you can't see anything, and yet you see everything. In the eyes of the stars, we are a microscopic point out there that will eventually pass away quickly, but this is not a cause for sadness. For me, it is a call to see beyond the superficial. (Anna)

The bigger context can be both about physical and imaginative space.

I would display a painting entitled 'Intergalactic Friends' by Oleg Litvinenko. The work belongs to the genre of magical realism. It shows things beyond the rational and realistic, emphasizing that humans exist in a broader context, much broader, dependent on the environment, nature and other people, and the magic that happens between us. (Żaneta)

Art also reveals the big picture inside of us.

It may be a completely crazy idea, but if I could choose a work that would be displayed in the hall of our Faculty, I would choose Kazimierz Malewicz's 'Black Square on a white background'. It is a seemingly simple work, even depreciated by some, but in my opinion of extraordinary value! Malewicz forces us to talk and discuss, he inspires, and shows that it is worth departing from patterns, choosing your own path (whether in art, life or management). Although, as he wrote himself, he exhibited an 'impression of objectlessness', this impression may become the beginning of some change – in the style of thinking, being, understanding. The black square against a white background proves that art can be a part of philosophy, so we should respect it, learn about it and look for values that can be used not only in our private life, but also in scientific and professional life. (Karolina)

Art poses some fundamental questions.

I think we need more reflections, questions, doubts and questions without ready-made answers. Paul Gauguin's painting 'Where do we come from? What are we? Where are we going?' does just that. (Eliza)

In the eye of some of my respondents, art teaches empathy.

I would love to see one (or the whole series) of the geometric paintings by Piotr Lutyński. The artist's vision was perfectly reflected in the setting of the works during the exhibition 'Buddha, Mars and the Deer'[5] at Bunkier Sztuki Gallery, where the Buddha was represented as the centre, to symbolize an enlightened being, surrounded by simple geometric arrangements with vivid colours (which are so characteristic of Lutyński). The geometric works are inspired by the aesthetic needs of animals. I think it would make us more compassionate and also relate to the artist's vision, which is full of tender irony...(Angelika)

Sometimes it does so quite forcefully.

Pola Dwurnik's 'Mercy!' Maybe it would make all of us rethink, before we hurt someone, before we unload our negativity or stress on another. (Kasia)

But, thankfully, art also helps to summon courage.

I would like to display one of my favourite paintings, 'The Wanderer above the Sea of Fog' by Caspar David Friedrich. It is about looking into the unknown 'sea of mists' with hope and composure, not knowing what the future will bring, but being aware that all the mists can be dispelled thanks to dedication and courage. (Chris)

Art can communicate a sense of connection – for example the

installation by Japanese artist Chiharu Shiota, 'Counting Memories', makes an electrifying impression of relation. The photos do not do it justice; they look quite dark. But the live experience is ineffable. The installations are made of yarn. Shiota creates a new installation for each place and none of them are ever repeated. The one that I think is the closest to what I would like to happen with the space where it would be exhibited is the installation 'Beyond Time', from Yorkshire Sculpture Park in Great Britain. This work of art evokes in me a feeling of possibilities and connections at the same time. Nothing happens without a reason, everything belongs somewhere. It makes me think of innocence, purity and omnipotence. The work is a mystery. The thicket, the concurrence triggers lots of echoes, reaching out to the viewers. (Joanna)

Art reminds of powerful moments in history – and of powerful women leaders.

Stefan Torelli's painting 'Allegory of Catherine II's victory over the Turks' represents the power of knowledge and progress leading us to a brighter future. Catherine the Great's victory over Turkey made Russia a superpower and the empress earned for herself the glory of being an enlightened ruler. (Kasia)

But history does not have to be just about rulers. It should also remind us of workers, especially women at work, who all too often tend to be forgotten about.

Two pictures together. The first is Jean Francois Millet's 'The Gleaners', which would show the hard work done by poor women in an almost empty field. The second is 'Indian summer' by Józef Chełmoński, showing a female farmer having a well-deserved rest after work in the field. Both works of art were criticized at the time they were first exhibited, because they were focusing on poor people – and, moreover, women, and were said to propagate a plebeian taste. But work is beautiful, and so is rest. (Ola)

It warns of the consequences of passivity.

I would choose Magdalena Abakanowicz's sculpture 'The Crowd'. The figures are in the shape of human bodies, but they do not have a face, that aspect of autonomy, one that most determines the characteristics of a person's personality. Without heads, the figures have no identity, cannot express themselves, and have no right to vote. This would make it clear how important it is not to lose oneself, not to become faceless. (Polina)

Thanks to art we are able to realize that there is much more to life than the ego.

I would choose a sculpture by Paige Bradley that impresses me and absorbs me very much – Expansion (Meditating woman). We all suffer from dilemmas that tear us in different directions. And yet there is something alive in us, in the inner space and emotions. This sculpture would encourage many to reflect on who we are and what we carry within us, beyond the shell of the ego. (Anna)

Cooperation by working for a common good is another important message. Return to 'normal' after the pandemic should be rooted in solidarity.

Evan M. Cohen's illustration, 'It is nice to be back together again', shows that it is important to strive for a common goal and that, thanks to solidarity, it is possible to create something valuable and beautiful. I think the illustration would be relevant especially after the pandemic and the return to 'normal'. (Magdalena)

Art opens our eyes to some timely truths.

I would exhibit a painting by René Magritte, 'Golconda'. It is difficult to clearly determine whether the depicted figures float, fall, or remain static – but regardless of this, they keep their distance from each other. Each character looks the same, does not interact with the environment, there is no place for relationships with others and individualism, and the windows of the buildings shown in the picture are covered and cut off from the outside world. The distance between people may also indicate more metaphorically a 'bubble' of security and remind us that our freedom ends where the freedom of another person begins. Until we ourselves start to pay attention to the world around us and the people around us, we will not know if we are rising and developing, we are falling, dragging others with us, or we are stagnant, indifferent and we are not able to change anything in reality (Aleksandra)

Some chose Banksy, not so much because he shows something, but, rather, because his art *does* something, moves the viewer to act.

I believe that we are moved by his art, it refers to emotions, it makes us think/ reflect, but it also mobilizes. That is why I would suggest making a 'creative space' in our main hall. On the walls there could be an exhibition of photos of Banksy's street art. They could change every month...In addition, there could be concerts, panels, meetings, and inspiring talks – there would be a space for development and dialogue where people would meet. (Anna)

But is it also important to find truth and beauty in the small things.

German graphic artist Christoph Niemann has a creative approach to ordinary things. It awakens curiosity and attention: 'Wow, how did he come up with it?', but also sensitivity to perceiving beauty in the things around us. I created a collage of the artist's works. (Marzena)

Among the students there were some who proposed a work of the arts or crafts that they themselves have made, or intend to make. Paweł wants to create something genuinely and vibrantly helpful.

I love gardening. I would create a living installation: shrubs and mushrooms. I would tear away the floor and make an orangery in the entire hall. People would be able to walk around the shrubs. This would give them peace and I would also be able to literally contribute to giving people air to breathe. (Paweł)

Several wanted to do a

> mural. At the very top there would be a book that people
> would reach out for. People visible in the mural would work
> together to reach for the book. This mural would show that
> cooperation and books are beautiful. This is what knowledge
> is all about. (Wera)

But it could also be just a simple pleasure of playing and sharing.

> I would offer one of my cat pictures. Many of us like to spend
> our free time on the Internet watching videos and photos
> with cute cats, and I would like to bring joy and happiness,
> a gift from the heart; that is my idea when I make these
> pictures. (Dominika)

The responses usually point out a specific artwork and propose
to place it within the space used by the respondent in the hope
that it will bring in some impressions, ideas or values. They
usually relate this influence to themselves and, in some cases,
to the wider community using the space. However, the stories
leave it at that – somewhat hopeful – note. In order to make use
of this hope more actively, something else is needed – concerted
action. Let's grab the imaginoscope and reach out to other
people!

7. Arrival: Enacting the imaginoscopic transmutation

7.1. The theatre of (social) life

Have you been one of the children playing astronauts, school or shop? I did all of that and more. It was so much fun to alternately be the saleswoman, trying to convince the recalcitrant customer to buy her fresh apples, the best ones she shall ever find in this market or, indeed, in the world – and the grumpy customer, complaining about everything and asking for an apple that will make the weather nice. Both roles had a pull of their own. One just felt what to say and do. When swapping roles you may have decided to be nice to the saleswoman but it somehow did not work that way. The game we played, back then, just had to have a grumpy customer in it. And the saleswoman would not take any shit readily. It was a battle of wits (and sometimes of rotten apples, too). You probably had your own customs and rules if you played shop as a child. But you may recognize the pull of the roles, the way they somehow put a spell on the player. That is something that professional actors, too, recognize, to a degree. The prominent Polish actor Janusz Gajos (2017) is one of many who speak of the magic of the theatre and impersonating a role is, at the best, a kind of interpersonal chemistry that happens 'when they all give up on themselves and become dolls that can animate themselves' (ibid., p. 218). Actors play roles on theatrical stages and in film studios and open-air plans. Children impersonate real and fictional characters as part of play. But roleplaying is far more common than just as a kind of art or children's play and the imaginoscope may help us to do so as imaginatively as possible, as is suitable in liminal conditions.

Theatre is an old art capable of making humans do and say what needs to be done and said, onstage – as well as offstage. In *As You Like It*, William Shakespeare says, through one of the characters:

> *All the world's a stage,*
> *And all the men and women merely players;*
> *They have their exits and their entrances,*
> *And one man in his time plays many parts* (Shakespeare, 2006, p. 227)

In his well-known book *The Presentation of Self in Everyday Life*, sociologist Erving Goffman (1990) presents ordinary members of society as performers of roles using different means of dramatic expression to communicate with and influence others. The social structure is made up of such roles that, when enacted, express the place of a person in society, and also have certain concrete effects, encoded in the structure. For example, a plainclothes policewoman showing her badge commands authority. Sometimes people give false performance in order to create an impression that is not supported by the actual position within the society. For example, a person may use complicated words to seem educated while he, in fact, is not. The theatricality of everyday life produces the Zeligs around us – as well as much less sympathetic figures.

One of the main differences between theatre on stage and in life is the role of the audience. The role of the audience in everyday social interactions is not passive: each member is playing a role of his or her own. The cashier in the grocery store plays a role, as do all the people standing in the queue, as well as the person unpacking the delivery of goods in the storeroom and the supplier of fresh produce. Everyone is playing a social role with everyone else as audience, involving the people present, but yet with another, much larger, audience in mind – society itself. We usually know who we are and what is expected of us.

Another difference between life and theatre concerns the formality of the performance. While many (if not all) theatrical performances have a script to follow, the performance of social roles is mainly about a tentative enactment and each social actor is adjusting her or his performance to fit in with how others receive it and to their own capabilities, goals and visions. There are, of course, more formalized procedures and sets of rules, especially for professional roles. But much of the content is based on tradition and interaction with others. There is also a wide, if not free, space for interpretation of enactment with roots in what has been culturally defined as 'acceptable', 'desired', or, indeed – 'recognizable', because the main point of the play of social roles is to facilitate collaboration and for that we need to be able to recognize who the other player is and what is expected of us in relation to him or her. The roles are constantly performed and improvised: 'every person who undertakes to play one of these roles plays it anew, tentatively' (Czarniawska-Joerges, 1992, p. 125).

The performance of social roles also involves negotiations

concerning the way in which they should be performed. They are rarely explicit and quite often spontaneous, yet usually quite strict. How can the expectations directed to the role we play be addressed? Is there much room for individual choice? What can we expect in return? All these questions are rooted in the context of culture and in social structures, which are more or less explicit. People usually 'get a feeling' about what they are 'supposed to do' when they grow up and become adults. They also have ideas about the audience and its reactions, only some of which are documented in the form of regulations, job descriptions or ethical codes. There are often real sanctions following the performance, and some are legally binding: misperformance can lead to a breach of relationships, withheld rewards or penalties of varying severity, from suspended payment to dismissal or even legal consequences. The rules change across space and time. For example, some 40 years ago Polish students used to feel obliged to help one another with everything, including sharing books, notes and helping each other during exams. Nowadays much of such help is considered dishonest and is even explicitly banned. Sometimes roles played by the same person conflict with each other and they may be, or not, structural or cultural means of dealing with such conflict. For example, in a small family business the role of boss and family member, for example, of the mother, may be at odds sometimes, if not constantly. However, most of us are able to deal with the inconsistences, challenges and uncertainties brought by the theatre of everyday life. Humans are quite proficient actors.

In these mundane roles played in workplaces, usual social settings and everyday organizations, social actors present considerable creativity and energy. This can be used to enrich social interactions, make people more sensitive towards one another – or to draw energy from people to fulfil a purpose imposed by someone or something else, such as profit or effectivity. People comply with exploitative management sometimes because the roles these managers play can be compelling and gripping. Heather Höpfl and Steve Linstead (1993) present an ethnographic study of a major airline company that requires emphatic displays of positive emotions at work from the flight attendants when addressing travellers, for several decades re-defined as customers. Such displays are staged and not always in line with their emotions or the real interactions between the employees and the others. But they lead to employees eagerly regarding themselves as actors. They often put so much dedication into the staging of these scenes that they feel burned out and empty when they get back home, devoid of energy to live their private lives. And yet they do the same thing over and over again – because they are expected to, and because these roles put their inner feelings at the disposal of management: this is a setting requiring emotional labour, they are employees with what Arlie Russell Hochschild (1983) labels a managed heart. Work in such a workplace may appear as similar to that on stage, argue Höpfl and Linstead (1993), but there are some fundamental differences. Unlike actors in a real theatre, the work of social actors is limited in both content and form; their task is to produce a clearly specified effect, not a multipurpose artistic experience. The performance attempts to hide all ambiguities (which theatre usually brings forward). The entire scope of feelings and experiences of the social actors is beyond the control of the actors and usually also the immediate supervisor. Nobody helps them to buffer and deal with the contradictions and conflicts of the performance but they are expected to do so privately and individually, using their own heart and soul. Instead of developing the artistic potential of the actors, it leads to their alienation. A theatrical actor, caught by the inability to play his or her role on stage, is said to be corpsing, failing in supporting the theatrical illusion. Corpsing poses a threat to the credibility of the whole performance. In workplaces sometimes a cumulative alienation leads to employee burnout, and to a growing aura of fake and emptiness of the whole performance. It threatens the dignity of all the participants of the interactions at work and sucks away joy. But work does not necessarily mean alienation. If respect for the actor's feelings is maintained and the awareness of the differences between the art of theatre and everyday roleplaying is understood and respected by management, the performance can be not only decent but beautiful and worthwhile.

An important step is to see and understand what theatre can do. Organization theorists Iain Mangham and Michael Overington (1987) propose a dramatic perspective to consciously use in work settings such as meetings.

> Theatre is an opportunity for mundane opportunities to be inspected as appearances in order to consider their meanings. As such, theatre creates space for awareness. This space and this experience, moreover, are available only in the performance itself and only then while the theatrical frame, the awareness of the frame on the part of audience and actors, is unquestioned. (ibid, p. 101)

In real theatre, the actors who enact the roles of characters and impersonate them may be gripped by the role but do not lose an awareness of being actors. Sometimes, like Janusz Gajos often does, actors on stage are both the role and the player at the same time: actors through which the role is speaking. The same is true about the audience; it may be drawn into the magic of the performance, may identify with the characters, but still be conscious, at some level, of it all being an illusion. That can be said to be the point of the enchantment of theatre: this dual presence, in the reality of the 'normal' world and the theatrical one simultaneously. Good theatre can bear both, and not spoil the spell. There are boundaries between the worlds obvious for everyone and as long as they are respected (and no corpsing occurs), they meet gracefully and gently in the theatrical space. Cinema does not always do that, especially if watched outside of the movie theatre. There may be a desire to cross over between the realms and to make people believe the enacted is in fact the same as the world they inhabit every day. Many children and some adults believe that what is happening in feature films is actually real. But cinema has its magic too, only it is not as immediately physical, not usually.

Iain Mangham and Michael Overington (1987) propose that not just the glamour of theatre but also the conscious ritual of drama be used in organizational settings. In other words, if we remember that what we partake in is a kind of play, the play gets more honest and also more humane. Dramatization can then be a useful organizational mindset, because it makes it possible for the participants to focus on something, a topic, such as the product, the strategy, as well as offering a way to enact the culture. It also helps to keep in mind that the performance must be able to 'attract' the audience in order to be convincing. Neither dramas performed in theatre nor those staged in organizations are actual performances unless there is an audience who takes them in – only rehearsals or, if done in full costume, dress rehearsals. The audience is part of the performance. In a real theatre, we know who the audience is, because it sits right in front of the stage. In the case of organizations, the social actors are each others' audience, but there are other audiences out there: clients, stakeholders, the media. They need to be made conscious and somehow addressed in order for the theatrical metaphor to work well. Finally, Mangham and Overington also point out that there is an artistic dimension to management and organizing. A skilful and conscious approach brings forward the aesthetic aspects of organizing and everyday life. American philosopher Kenneth Burke created the famous dramatistic pentad (1945), which 'treats language and thought primarily as modes of action' (p. xxii). It can be kept in mind in order to stay conscious of all these important aspects with the help of the following categories:

> ...Act, Scene, Agent, Agency, Purpose. In a rounded statement about motives, you must have some word that names the act (names what took place, in thought or deed), and another that names the scene (the background of the act, the situation in which it occurred); also, you must indicate what person or kind of person (agent) performed the act, what means or instruments he used (agency), and the purpose. Men may violently disagree about the purposes behind a given act, or about the character of the person who did it, or how he did it, or in what kind of situation he acted; or they may even insist upon totally different words to name the act itself. But be that as it may any complete statement about motives will offer some kind of answers to these five questions: what was done (act), when or where it was done (scene), who did it (agent), how he did it (agency), and why (purpose). (p. 15)

These aspects do not require a theatre building. The British theatre director Peter Brook (1990) presents four modes of theatre: Deadly, which is artificial and hollow, even though it creates pleasure; Holy – theatre that makes the invisible visible; Rough, that is down to earth and forges a link between spectators and actors; and Immediate, which occurs when the audience reacts to the happening unravelling on stage. Theatre can be more or less complex, more or less elaborate and structured. However, according to Brook, it all begins with a person walking across the empty space, while someone else is watching. The empty is the bare stage: the minimum setting for a theatrical performance to take place. It offers the potential to make theatre happen, an invitation to fill it with the content.

When we are persuaded to believe in this truth, then the theatre and life are one. This is a high aim. It sounds like hard work. To play needs much work. But when we experience the work as play, then it is not work anymore. A play is play (Brook, 1990, p. 157).

Everyday life can be seen in the very same way, if performed as a set of roles, consciously and deliberately. One imaginoscopic tool that can help us with learning this mindset for contexts outside of the theatre building is roleplaying games. Jerzy Kociatkiewicz (2000) narrates a roleplaying experiment, which was organized with the aim of understanding the creative learning of organizational roles. The physical space, as well as the rules and scenarios, were left purposefully open-ended, based on Brook's idea of the empty space. The sessions centred around the idea of creation, with only two states defined, both beyond the space of the players' roles: the initial nothingness and the something-ness to emerge as a result of the session. The roles and the characters emerged together with the realities the players created together. Both cooperation and rivalry appeared and some structures began to emerge, out of tentative relationships between the characters and the rules and features on which the other participants agreed. Kociatkiewicz concludes that a social organization slowly emerged from the mixture of symbols and relationships that the participants used to fill the original emptiness.

And this brings us back to children's play. The play usually contains at least some initial rules; for example, when you play grocery store, you need at least a saleswoman (or –man) and a customer. There needs to be an interaction focused on selling and buying. Finally, there has to be a product, or many products. The rest can be improvised, even though there usually are rules concerning the improvisation, such as the humorous banter that was a recurring feature in the game I used to play as a child. But just as on Brook's empty stage – it is play. It can be taken in different directions, it can take the children in different directions. When I recall these games, I have those vivid scenes in front of me: the other kids, the rituals, but also the characters we played, the weeds and wild plants we played with but also the cabbages, onions, leeks that it symbolized for us. The pieces of paper that were cash (no credit cards yet in those days). Both the actual props and the illusion we created of them. Play is indeed both mundane and magical. The imaginoscope, used on social interactions, can make us revive it.

Here are a few guidelines on how to invite the theatrical dimension into everyday life with the help of the imaginoscope.

- Visit the theatre with a friend. Enjoy the play and take time to discuss it with your friend afterwards. Which roles were played well and which were less convincing? Why? What persuaded each of you of the credibility and veracity of the characters impersonated on stage?
- Adopt a theatrical frame of mind and watch a speech by a politician or businessperson. Think like a theatrical critic. Was it a good or poor performance? Why? How could it have been performed more artistically, more creatively, more convincingly? Allow yourself to be as creative and imaginative as you wish. Think in terms of a Shakespearean play, portraying one of the old kings!
- Next time you go shopping or perform some other minor interactive task, consider the theatrical dimension of the interaction. How do you mark entering the role? Who is your audience? Who is your co-player? (it can be the same person) How do you know what to say, how to act? What influence do your words and acts have on the others when you are in this role?
- Next time you perform some minor interactive task, make it more creative and more imaginative and, at the same

time, respectful and considerate to the other social actors! Be witty, dramatic in a kind and social way, make the co-actors smile, brighten their (and your) day!

7.2. Practice: To stage a play

Imagine that a theatrical play was created about the current stage of your life. What is its title? What genre of theatre is it? What is your role in this play?

My students focused on the roles they played as university students. Many were primarily interested in the quest for knowledge.

The play would be called 'Romance with Knowledge'. I would be one of the many heroes and heroines who do not play the main role, but who are in love with Knowledge (the main character), not necessarily jealous of each other but not always cooperating, either. I would be a devoted lover who wants to be as close to Knowledge as possible and does lots of things, some heroic and some funny. (Karolina)

Here is another romance with knowledge, albeit a more turbulent one:

The title of my theatre play would be 'An Italian Marriage, or Breakups and Returns in Three Acts'. The plot of the performance would be a romance between me (just an average student) and science (the object of my love). This romance, as befits an Italian marriage, would be stormy – full of break-ups and returns, quarrels for life and death and passionate nights. It will all end well, with a lot of positive emotions. And although disappointment came sometimes, I still abide, isn't this what true love is like? (Gabriela)

Kara's romantic comedy has culture rather than knowledge as

the main character:

> The title of the play would be: 'A few words about Culture...' It would be a comedy and it would be funny. Culture is omnipotent, she can be and do anything. Her followers just need to open their mind and experience. But do they realize it?! My role would be that of a dreamer, following Culture (and watching people following her). (Kara)

Some, like Marta, chose to frame the drama as a fantastic or fairy-tale scenario. Marta, however, proposes an innovative interactive ending.

> The performance would be entitled The Art Of /Without a Choice and it would be a tragedy. It would tell about a gloomy kingdom in which the subjects have no influence on the decisions of the king, they are left to themselves. He does not even react when they have to deal on their own with terrible monsters lurking outside the city walls. However, they fight bravely, although they are divided and, for many, it ends in defeat. Some are not brave enough, others are lazy and lack perseverance, and still others have insufficient sword skills. Not working together, they stand little chance. They are overwhelmed with sorrow and intense fear for their future. My role in the play would be to play one of my subjects, a bit lost but stubbornly facing the adversities. There would be an open ending: each time the play is performed my character, together with the audience, decides if she had succeeded or not. (Marta)

A number of persons addressed the unusual situation of the lockdown. Some framed it as a tragedy, others as comedy. Klaudia chose tragicomedy.

A Comedy of Online Errors. The play would present the difficulties due to online teaching during the pandemic. It is difficult and even exasperating for all of us – both students and teachers. Lack of physical contact results in numerous errors, most often on the part of students, who expect interactions that are not possible with such a system. There are also crises, such as a lack of understanding on the part of the teachers, who sometimes overwhelm students with tasks that often take hours, even days, to perform...My role would be that of narrator / observer. I do not get involved in any disputes with teachers regarding their way of conducting classes. I know that the situation is complicated for both parties. So I would not play the role of the aggrieved party, the guilty party, or the initiating conflict. The role of a compassionate, annoyed and amused narrator / observer would be appropriate for me. (Klaudia)

Our times seem to invite dark comedies. Here is another example.

It would be entitled Young and Tired. The viewer would be free to laugh and perceive the play as a comedy, there will be lots of slapsticks and silly jokes in it. But the actors would feel that this is indeed a tragedy. A group of young people get increasingly bored, tired and disheartened on the stage. They make silly faces, they do silly things, they have idiotic conversations with one another, with computers, then with chairs and other stuff. They would roll over on stage, stumble, trip over. I would be one of the silly companions, but somebody who tries to take care of the others who feel lost. Sometimes I would succeed but most often I would just end up doing very silly things and looking daft. I would be alternately tender and sarcastic, lyrical one moment and cynical the next. (Edyta)

The satirical mood led some of the respondents into imaginative territories reminding me at the same time of Beckett and 1970s TV series.

> A theatre play about my life right now would be entitled 'Last Hope'. I think that genre would lie on the verge of epic and satire. The plot would depict one night of a collective cramming marathon with a minimum of sleep, gradually turning cheerful students into mindless zombies. The only hope would be coffee with a lot of caffeine, but it's all gone by now, people have drunk it all and no one is able to find real coffee in the entire building. A group of persistent heroes, trying to save their friends from total mutation, would look for a vending machine with the best and strongest coffee in the building, which would save the students from zombification. I would play the role of the wise guide to the vending machines, as I know where they all are and which are best to avoid. (Martyna)

The epic form was quite popular. Here one of the respondents reveals the plot of a heroic play.

> The title of the play would be: Looking for the future. It would be an epic, and it begins with the future being officially cancelled. A group of young people on a mission, ready to fight the system, for women's rights, for animal rights, for the climate. Against politicians, against big business. They face many difficult tests and tribulations and the enemy is much more powerful than they thought. They lose many fights but they believe that there is a victory somewhere, ultimately, and that they can achieve it. If not, there is no future. No planet. They are very brave and sometimes quite cunning. I would be one of the fighters, always ready to face the danger. But I would also be looking for inspiration, in

books, at the university. (Marta)

A tragic plot may, sometimes, have warmer undertones.

The title would be: 'Þetta reddast – everything will work out in the end'. It would be a tragedy, but with a twist. The tragic part of the plot would pertain to the quest for understanding of art, and for the gaining of some higher experience by young people. But there would also be farcical elements, in the portrayal of how people pursue the goal. There would be no element of conflict in the play, or good-evil juxtaposition. This is deliberate. The main task is to focus on adventures that affect the main characters. However, some of them are tragic and some comical. The characters are complex and unruly; they like to choose their own path, not fully realizing the consequences of this choice. Therefore, they encounter many difficulties on their way that they do not always know how to deal with. Often their actions backfire, putting them in very comical situations. The play would differ from all films or series that show studies as something superficial, focusing primarily on the 'fun' and interpersonal relations. My play would also include science, and art – things that are elusive but really important to the students. This play would also present a true image of our times: dynamic, unpredictable, absurd, with elements of black humour, full of doubts. The title is significant. It has a positive tone because, despite everything the characters have to deal with, they find themselves in this situation together. Therefore, the name of the play would refer more to an epilogue that could be epic or romantic; taking place in an undefined future in which the fates of the characters are becoming less and less absurd. They find their place in the world, not necessarily related to the field of our studies, but they remember about science and art, and that is a good thing. (Aleksandra)

Some respondents propose imaginative dramatic forms, such as an absurdist pantomime:

> The Box: A pantomime. The performance tells the story of a group of young people locked in a huge box with transparent walls. The box is tall, but it does not have a ceiling. The goal of the people inside is to get out of it. There are two ways: you can exit through the door on one of the walls, or climb up perfectly smooth walls and exit at the top. After a brief fight, a group decides to leave through the door. Those who remain are less combative but have to face a whole range of other emotions, which are sometimes very strong, and they solve many problems to climb the walls and get out. Sometimes an outsider comes in and helps them in some way. Some form groups and work together, while others act alone. And still others climb on the back of other persons. It is a story about emotions: joy, euphoria, sadness, frustration, anger ...In this play, I am one of the people who chose to stay in the box. The walls are not my problem. My problem is the ceiling, or lack thereof. It is not about imprisonment, it is about persistence. Do I know this? What are the real limitations? This is what the play explores. But, at the end of the play, I manage to get out of the box. (Weronika)

Yuliia imagined a performance.

> The play, entitled 'From I to I', is a plastic mono-performance (i.e. a performance with one actor) with elements of improvisation. Plastic means that it would include body art (not just dance), which conveys the meaning in a special way: it emphasizes the monologue, or protests against it. My role in this play is, of course, the lead (and the solo). I am also, at the same time, the director and the author, because I improvise. I take responsibility for what I create. My role

is to show who I am now and who I become. And between two different incarnations there is improvisation, looking for myself. And this is the most important – the in-between. (Yuliia Savytska)

The responses are narrative snippets that offer some general ideas about the roles the authors believe themselves to play in their everyday life, and the wider context in which that takes place. They could all be developed into a complete play that can be performed on a stage. And that would be interesting, would it not? However, this is not quite what this book proposes that we do at this stage of the quest with the imaginoscope.

Rather, after having pondered the role and the play, the imaginoscope indicates that we now enact something in real life, something that would manifest the dreams and insights that the imaginoscope has helped us to collect on the way. It does not have to be anything major, like moving to another country or changing jobs. In fact, it is rather advisable to create something small and on the side of life's major highways, and to see what grows out of it. From the stories I have heard in the field where I do ethnographic research – cooperative organizers and ecopreneurs – I gather that such small side projects taking place in sheltered poetic spaces, fuel encounters and ongoing discussions make collective dreams manifest and possible to realize. In other words, this is how many of the existing and viable alternative organizations in my field originally emerged. An eco-touristic enterprise began as a group of people meeting after the death of their teacher and discussing his ideas of a living museum, pondering if something like that can be done in real life. An eco-bazaar materialized as a result of a group of friends going to the cinema together and then chatting about things they saw on film that they would like to do together. A cooperative hostel began as a group of anarchists meeting and talking about good and bad workplaces. So this is what the book proposes that we do now: collect a group of potentially interested friends and organize something of a roleplaying circle, dedicated to the discussion of a common interest that you wish to be developed into something more solid, together with others. It may be a group of people walking in the woods and discussing ecological issues for the future. Or a book club talking about implications for the future that can be found in literature. Or a poetry club, sharing poetic inspirations for the future. Or a group of friends dedicated to talking about food, sharing thoughts and ideas of ecological agriculture and getting in touch with local farmers. Or a circle of cinema-goers, looking for ideas of the future that can be found in film, be it old or modern. When I began to write this book, I started a discussion circle dedicated to art and organizing. I contacted the students whose responses appear in this book and invited them to join in regular short meetings, online for now (due to the still active COVID-19 pandemic). A group of people were interested and so we meet and chat about what art can teach us about themes that I propose before each session, such as animals or work. We then consider the implications this has for organizers and organizations. We still do this one year afterwards, even though most of them have since graduated and have other jobs and lives outside of the university. Whatever your imaginoscopic roleplaying group will be dedicated to, please keep in mind two important rules, which help to give structure (something that may be very important when the time comes for it to develop into something more solid): you have to have relatively stable roles in the group, which do not have to be tied to specific persons, and there has to be a regular time assigned for the meetings. The roles can be basic but they need to organize participation, for example: moderator, discussant, host. The participants can swap roles regularly and new roles can be introduced. The schedule does not have to be very tight, but it is good to meet once a week or once a fortnight. Too long periods of time without anything happening threaten the crystallization process of such elusive structures. It also helps to use a sheltered or special space, a heterotopia, such as a favourite café, or a place in the park, and switch off all mobile phones for the duration of the meetings. In times of lockdowns it is, of course, not possible, so Zoom or Skype has to do. It is, however, a good idea to introduce something symbolically special into the online space, such as asking the participants to share an image of artwork, or show the current view from their window. You need to feel safe and free to be imaginative. Therefore the group should have no concrete end and be formed outside of any existing structures. Our art and organizing discussion group takes place entirely in our free time and has no connection to academic institutions. The majority of the participants are done with their studies.

Grab the imaginoscope together, meet regularly and see what emerges. If, like some of the organizers in my field, you start having vivid dreams about things that can be done, take them seriously and test them in practice. One of the organizers dreamed of a building and realized that she can now, together with friends, look for funding to start an agrotouristic social enterprise. Another kept dreaming of tomatoes which drove her to make friends with a local farmer, who became a key co-organizer. Dreams often show the way in the liminal space.

8. Coda: So what now?

Our times tend to keep at hand a set of ready rapid, automatic categories for everything, which usually come in stark binary oppositions. It is always either this or the other, never *and – and*. Whenever a third alternative appears and acquires a transitory status it is swiftly re-categorized into one of the originals. Contemporary times abhor a synthesis. The category of 'androgyne', for example, all but disappeared in the new century, and yet it used to be a powerful idea of a synthesis of genders and sexualities. The primordial Greek god Eros was an androgyne. Numerous cultures, including Western ones in the former century, used to have a space and even times to celebrate androgyny. It is not a male-female dichotomy; it is not non-binary. It is not static. Its lack of definition is at its heart; it is about complex human dynamics: human beings cannot be reduced to chromosomes, and there is a whole spectrum of hormones at play which change during our life. It is also about aesthetics, desire, attraction. Androgyny as a process is common enough but it is rare as a path of life, because, due to its complexity, it is difficult to embrace it and use as a role template. It is not a temporary state that needs to be 'fixed' or corrected. In most cases it does not call for surgery or drug therapy because it is not transitory, and it is not a problem. The problem is patriarchy, which defines active social participation and success on male terms and aims at ridding society of female aspects, such as non-linearity, awareness of embodiment, focus on care. A society without women is a morbid fantasy. A world without androgyny is devoid of fantasy, art, eroticism and poetry. It is a rhetorical prison of imposed forms which is being erected in the name of coherence. The same things apply to other and-ands, such as bi-culturals (who now tend to be categorized as foreigners or immigrants) or people with mixed conservative-liberal worldviews (who tend to be seen as centrists). Without a synthesis, the categorical oppositions form neither a thesis nor an antithesis, and they do not come together, they just order and re-order reality without creating anything new, re-shuffle neatly what already exists according to a given algorithm. They do not teach – they are just divisive.

In better times, hybrids, or explorers of borderline realities, are very much appreciated, because we bring challenge, amusement and hope. They are the Marco Polos, the Bilbos, the shamans, who bring new elements into the existing culture, inspiring renewal and raising questions. In worse times, the choices seem, for most people and organizations, to be limited to avoiding the greater evil. In such binary cultures there is no place for hybrids. In the best case, they are unseen; in worse circumstances – they are ostracized, marginalized, even removed with violence. Hybrids are always rare, even unique, they never form the mainstream, and are neither obvious nor easily recognizable. It takes effort to bring them into a cultural reality, but it is worth it. They offer cultural and social amalgamates, poems of light, songs of innocence and experience, genre and gender fluidity, the ambivalent, ambiguous and fluctuating, with the same pulse as dreams. Their fate provides the most precise, accurate barometer of the times. The day when hybrids are welcome again and people start seeing them, on that day we can be certain that austerity, the war on diversity and abundance – on the stuff of life itself – is over. But to get there, we need to restrain divisive patterning, stop the obsessive and automatic ordering of reality into neat oppositions. First and foremost, we need a pause.

John Keats's negative capability – the ability to refrain from immediate categorization and to embrace uncertainty and mystery – is the opposite of allowing patterns to form automatically in our minds. It allows us to flow with perception. What people call genius is not located within the individual but in the co-flowing with things around us. In a way, it can be seen as doing nothing. Nothing: no adopting, no adapting, no focusing, no contributing, no presenting. No hard work, and, above all, no impact. It is silence, being the straw through which the water flows. Wherever it takes. No resistance, no effort, no authorship. No stillness, no harmony, no relevance. But it is neither passive nor depersonalized. Quite the contrary: it is a tremendous effort and dedication, requiring will, love, practise and wisdom, which may sometimes allow a flow much bigger than our individual selves to flood through us. It allows us to use the flow to actively shape reality, to create things small and big. It is hard to say what these flows consist of, but their workings spread from human to human through stories.

We need more stories, different stories, not the ones of heroic individuals and progress but about togetherness, beauty and truth. They will probably be incoherent at first, which presents some serious difficulty for a person not endowed with negative capability. Psychologist Daniel Kahneman (2012) observes that coherence automatically induces 'the cognitive ease that causes us to accept a statement as true' (p. 87). Yet, social scientist and theologian Przemysław Piątkowski (2021) remarks that coherence is not the same thing as truth. We need to find the patience in ourselves, through the practising of negative capability and the telling of liminal stories, to allow for incoherence through which a new truth will appear. Leonard Cohen (1992) sings in his song 'Anthem' about everything being fractured, thus allowing light to enter.

Poets and storytellers have the ability to address this light coming in. It takes both courage, experience and power. Not everything that glitters is light, most of it is some other surface reflecting it: gold, prestige (a word meaning 'illusion' in the original Latin), or, worse still, a sudden flash of blinding darkness. Wisdom is necessary to tell the difference between them all. For this task we need tribal storytellers, and the powerful archetypes they use in their stories. Let us bring back eldership instead of condemning old age to senility, uselessness and unproductivity. Society without eldership grows senile and becomes demented due to lack of living memory, reflection and forgiveness. Let us welcome back the eternal child, with its dreams and its innocence. We care so much for children, abhor violence done to them, strongly condemn, even demonize child molesters. But what do we do, as society, to the inner child in each of us? We violate it, we break it, we ravage its innocence and only then are we disposed to call someone an adult when she is no longer prone to looking up at the sky without reason, or to trust strangers without hesitation. What we now call 'adulthood' is violence done to our inner child. Advancement and social success only comes to those who are able to crush and suffocate their inner child: its empathy, its joy, simplicity and sincerity. Increasingly, our organizations and institutions come to be managed by those who either are sociopaths or can make themselves behave like ones (Boddy, 2011). Someone who cannot stomach another's suffering is considered to be made of stuff too weak to hold a position of power or, indeed, to be taken too seriously; he is just 'too sensitive' (Szpunar, 2018). It has become something of a test – to murder the child we still are, at heart. We need these and other archetypes: the lover, the king (male and female), the trickster.

Carl Gustav Jung (1968) saw archetypes as riverbeds waiting to be filled with contents: stories, characters, ideas. Perhaps they are something even more corporeal: veins in the collective body of humanity. In our times they are being pumped full with the formaldehyde of financial flow; petrifying, embalming, making the dead body look presentable. The body is dead because it is dried of the blood of invigorating stories. But the body of humanity can be resurrected. The imaginoscope can serve as a *passe-partout* to open up the veins for the flow of archetypical tales. Such tales work magic, they are the flow of life, the stuff that human beings are made on.

This is not an easy endeavour. It takes time and effort but most of all, it requires commitment. To make a vow to stories of life and persevere faithfully, ready to encounter injustice, lack of appreciation, loss of prestige (do we really need a life based on illusion?). It is a difficult but lovely way to take, difficult but graceful. Theologian Dietrich Bonhoeffer (1995) speaks of costly grace. The Gospels recount Jesus' parable of the pearl of great price: the kingdom of Heaven is like the merchant who sold all of his goods in order to buy the pearl (Matthew 13: 45-46; Thomas 76). Real grace is costly, it demands devotion, determination, discipline. It is the door at which one has to knock. One has to be ready to give up much in order to get it. Even, if it comes to it, as it did for Bonhoeffer himself, his life. But let us not allow it to come to this, for ourselves, for others, for the planet. Each on her own, we cannot do much to resist the deadly dynamic of the dying system. But together, with grace, and with time – we can.

Having time

To have time is to look up
at the sky at night, to the stars.
The light up there
is millions years old. The stars, the darkness,
myself, all strung on the string
of very old light. It
may go on for millions more years
or forever.
(Monika Kostera, 2021)

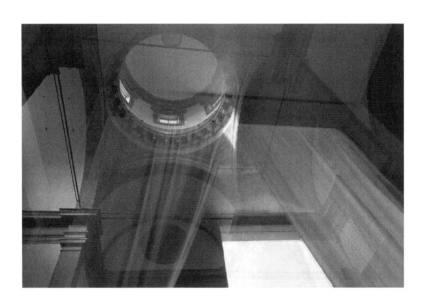

Bibliography

Andersen, Hans Christian (2016) 'The emperor's new suit', in: *The complete works of Hans Christian Andersen, 1805-1875*. Hastings: Delphi.

Ashby, W. Ross (1958) 'Requisite variety and its implications for the control of complex systems', *Cybernetica* ,11/ 2, p. 83-99.

Bachelard, Gaston (1969a) *The poetics of space*. Boston: Beacon Press.

Bachelard, Gaston (1969b) *The poetics of reverie: Childhood, language, and the cosmos*. Boston: Beacon Press.

Bachelard, Gaston (2013) *Intuition of the instant*. Evanston: Northwestern University Press.

Bauman, Zygmunt (2012) 'Times of interregnum', *Ethics and Global Politics*, 5/1, p. 49-56.

Benjamin, Walter (1999) *The Arcades project*. Cambridge, Mass.: Belknap Press of Harvard University Press.

Berardi, Franco 'Bifo' (2018) *Breathing: Chaos and poetry*. South Pasadena: Semiotext(e).

Berger, John (1972) *Ways of seeing*. London: Penguin.

Berthoin Antal, Ariane (2014) 'When arts enter organizational spaces: Implications for organizational learning', In: P. Meusburger (Series Ed.) & Ariane Berthoin Antal, P. Meusburger, & L. Suarsana (Eds.) *Knowledge and space: Vol. 6. Learning organizations: Extending the field*. Dordrecht: Springer, p. 177-201.

Bettelheim, Bruno (1976) *Uses of enchantment*. London: Thames and Hudson.

Blake, William (2013) 'Auguries of Innocence', in: *Complete Works*. Hastings: Deplhi.

Blake, William (2019) *Jerusalem: The emanation of the giant Albion*. Accessed on 14.01.2019 at http://ld.johanesville.net/blake-18-jerusalem-the-emanation-of-the-giant-albion?page=8

Blakely, Grace (2020) *The corona crash: How the pandemic will change capitalism.* London: Verso.

Boddy, Clive R. (2011) *Corporate psychopaths: Organizational destroyers.* London: Palgrave Macmillan.

Bonhoeffer, Dietrich (1995) *The cost of discipleship.* New York: Touchstone.

Brook, Peter (1990) *The empty space.* Harmondsworth: Penguin.

Bruner, Jerome (1991) 'The narrative construction of reality'. *Critical Inquiry*, 18(1), s. 1-21.

Bruner, Jerome S. (1990) *Acts of meaning.* Cambridge, Mass.: Harvard University Press.

Burke, Kenneth (1945) *A grammar of motives.* Berkeley: University of California Press.

Campbell, Joseph (1988a) *Myths to live by: How we recreate ancient legends in our daily lives to release human potential.* New York-Toronto-Sydney-Auckland: Bantam Books.

Campbell, Joseph (1988b) *The inner reaches of outer space: Metaphor as myth and as religion.* New York: Harper & Row.

Campbell, Joseph (2012) *The Hero with a thousand faces.* Novato: New World Library.

Cohen, Leonard (1992) 'Anthem', *The Future.* Sony Music Entertainment.

Cohen, Leonard (2006) *The book of longing.* New York: Harper & Collins.

Czarniawska, Barbara (1999) *Interviews, narratives and organizations.* Göteborg: GRI-report.

Czarniawska-Joerges, Barbara (1991) 'Culture is the medium of life'. in: Peter J. Frost, Larry F. Moore, Meryl Reis Louis, Craig C. Lundberg and Joanne Martin (ed.) *Reframing organizational culture.* Newbury Park: SAGE, p. 285-297.

Czarniawska-Joerges, Barbara (1992) *Exploring complex organizations: A cultural perspective.* Newbury Park: Sage.

De Certeau, Michel (1988) *The practice of everyday life.* Berkeley: University of California Press.

Denzin, Norman K. (2002) *Interpretive interactionism.* London: Sage.

Deslandes, Ghislain (2020) 'Weak theology and organization studies', *Organization Studies,* 41(1) 127–139.

French, Robert (2001) '"Negative capability": Managing the confusing uncertainties of change', *Journal of Organizational Change Management,* 14/5, 480-492.

Gabriel, Yiannis (2020) 'Kafka and the COVID-10 epidemic: Why the sirens' silence is more deadly than their song', *Leadership,* 16(3), p. 320-330.

Gajos, Janusz (2017), in: Janusz Gajos, Katarzyna Jabłońska and Andrzej Luter (interview) 'Stop! Właśnie tak ma być', *Więź* 3/669, p. 209-219.

Garfinkel, Harold (1967) *Studies in ethnomethodology.* Englewood Cliffs: Prentice-Hall.

Goffman, Erving (1990) *The presentation of self in everyday life.* London: Penguin.

Goscinny, René and Jean-Jacques Sempé (2020) *Le petit Nicolas.* Retrieved 15.10.2020 from http://www.petitnicolas.com/

Gramsci, Antonio (1971) *Selections from the Prison Notebooks.* (ed. Quintin Hoare and Geoffrey Nowell Smith) London: Lawrence & Wishart.

Guillet de Monthoux, Pierre (1993) *Det sublimas konstnärliga ledning: Estetik, konst och företag.* Stockholm: Nerenius & Santérus.

Guillet de Monthoux, Pierre (1998) *Konstföretaget: Mellan spektakelkultur och kulturspektakel.* Stockholm: Korpen.

Handke, Peter (1987) 'Song of childhood', retrieved on 14.10.2020 from http://www.reverse-angle.com/deutsch/filme/katalog/timeline/ww-1/wingsofdesire/wod-song-of-childhood.htm

Hieronimus, Gilles (2020) 'Comment sortir sans s'en sortir?', in : Adele Van Reeth (ed.) *Les chemins de la philosophie.* Radio France Culture, retrieved on 9.11.2020 from https://www.franceculture.fr/emissions/les-chemins-de-la-philosophie/

confines-avec-gaston-bachelard-14-comment-sen-sortir-sans-sortir

Hillman, James (1989) *The essential James Hillman: A Blue Fire.* London: Routledge.

Hillman, James (2017) *The soul's code: In search of character and calling.* New York: Ballantine Books.

Hochschild, Arlie Russell (1983) *The managed heart: Commercialization of human feeling.* Berkeley: University of California Press.

Höpfl, Heather (1995) 'Organizational rhetoric and the threat of ambivalence'. *Studies in Cultures, Organizations and Societies,* 1/2, 175-187.

Höpfl, Heather and Stephen Linstead (1993) 'Passion and performance: Suffering and the carrying of organizational roles', in: Stephen Fineman (ed.) *Emotion and organization.* London: Sage, p. 76-93.

Jarmusch, Jim (2003) *Coffee and Cigarettes.* Hollywood: United Artists.

Jung, Carl Gustav (1980) The archetypes and the collective unconscious, in: Hubert Read (ed.) *The collected works of C. G. Jung.* Vol. 9. Princeton: Princeton University Press.

Kahneman, Daniel (2012) *Thinking, Fast and Slow.* London: Penguin Books.

Keats, John (1958) The letters of John Keats, H E Rollins (ed), Cambridge: Cambridge University Press.

Kociatkiewicz, Jerzy (2000) 'Dreams of time, times of dream', *Studies in Cultures, Organizations, and Societies* 6/1: 71-86.

Kociatkiewicz, Jerzy and Monika Kostera (2015) 'Into the labyrinth: Tales of organizational nomadism', Organization Studies, 36(1) 55-71.

Kofta, Mirosław and Anna M. Rędzio (2020) (eds) *Poczucie kontroli i niepewność: Konsekwencje dla rozumienia świata społecznego.* Warszawa: Liberi Libri.

Kostera, Monika (2016) *Oneiropeia.* Liverpool: Erbacce.

Kostera, Monika (2021) *Iotas*. Retrieved on 11.04.2021 from http://www.kostera.pl/Iotas.htm

Kostera, Monika and Joanna Średnicka (2016) 'Poezja i zarządzanie: Inspiracje dla menedżera humanisty', in: Monika Kostera and Bogusław Nierenberg (eds) Komunikacja społeczna i zarządzanie humanistyczne, s. 151-168.

Koźmiński, Andrzej K. and Krzysztof Obłój (1989) *Zarys teorii równowagi organizacyjnej*. Warszawa: PWE, for a more contemporary approach, incorporating some of the insights from the cultural turn in organization studies.

Latour, Bruno (2005) *Reassembling the social: An introduction to actor-network theory*. Oxford: Oxford UP.

Le Guin, Ursula K. (1995) *Four ways to forgiveness*. New York: HarperCollins.

Le Guin, Ursula K. (2014) 'Speech in acceptance of the national book foundation medal for distinguished contribution to American letters', *Ursula K. Le Guin,* accessed on 3.04.2021 at https://www.ursulakleguin.com/nbf-medal

Letiche, Hugo (2000) 'Phenomenal complexity theory as informed by Bergson', *Journal of Organizational Change Management*, 13/6, p. 545-557.

Letiche, Hugo (2021) 'Prologue to filmic research(ing)', in: Monika Kostera and Cezary Wozniak (eds) *Aesthetics, organization, and humanistic management*. New York: Routledge, pp. 217-234.

Mangham, Iain L. and Michael A. Overington (1987) *Organizations as theatre: A social psychology of dramatic appearances*. Chichester: John Wiley.

Mitchell, Kirsty (2018) *Wonderland*. Exhibition (2018-2019) at Stockholm Fotografiska, retrieved 17.10.2020 from https://www.fotografiska.com/sto/en/exhibition/wonderland/

Moriceau, Jean-Luc (2018) 'Écrire le qualitatif: écriture réflexive, écriture plurielle, écriture performance', *Revue Internationale de Psychosociologie et de Gestion des Comportements*

Organisationnels, ESKA, 24 (57), p. 45-67.

Morin, Edgar (1990) *Introduction à la pensée complexe*. Paris : ESF éditeur.

Morin, Edgar (2020) *Changeons de voie: Les* leçons *de coronavirus*. Paris: Denoël.

Morin, Edgar (2020) *Changeons de Voie: Les* leçons *de coronavirus*. Paris: Denoël.

Péju, Pierre (1981) *La petite fille dans la forêt des contes*. Paris : Robert Laffont.

Péju, Pierre (1981) *La petite fille dans la forêt des contes*. Paris : Robert Laffont.

Piątkowski, Przemysław (2021) 'The gospel of St. John', essay, Elgin: Domuni Universitas.

Shakespeare, William (2006) *As you like it*. London: Arden.

Simpson, Peter, Robert French and Charles E. Harvey (2002) 'Leadership and negative capability', *Human Relations*, 55/10, 1209–1226.

Smircich, Linda (1983) 'Concepts of culture and organizational analysis'. *Administrative Science Quarterly* 28/3, p. 339 – 358.

SSE Art Initiative (2020) *Art Initiative*. Retrieved on 26.10.2020 from https://www.hhs.se/en/outreach/sse-initiatives/art-initiative/

Standing, Guy (2019) *Plunder of the commons: A manifesto for sharing public wealth*. London: Pelican.

Streeck, Wolfgang (2017) *How will capitalism end? Essays on a failing system*. London: Verso.

Szpunar, Magdalena (2018) *(Nie)potrzebna wrażliwość*. Kraków: Wydawnictwo IDMiKS.

Theoderich (1986) *Theoderich:* Guide to the Holy Land, ed. by Ronald G. Musto. New York: Italica.

Tikkun (2020) 'Current thinking from Rabbi Lerner', retrieved on 10.11.2020 from https://www.tikkun.org/rabbi-michael-lerner

Turner, Victor (1970) *The forest of symbols: Aspects of Ndembu ritual.* Ithaca: Cornell University Press.

Uncivilization: The Dark Mountain manifesto (2014) The Dark Mountain Project.

Van Interson, Ad, Stewart Clegg and Arne Carlsen (2017) 'Ideas are feelings first: Epiphanies in everyday workplace creativity', *M@n@gement,* 3/20, p. 221-238.

Venkatesh, Alladi (1999) 'Why do you shop? (a conversation with Judith Wilske followed by a photo essay)', *Consumption, Markets and Culture,* 3(4), p. 297-330, DOI:10.1080/10253866. 1999.9670342

Weick, Karl (1995) *Sensemaking in organizations.* London: Sage.

Weick, Karl (2006) 'The role of imagination in the organizing of knowledge', *European Journal of Information Systems,* 15, s. 446-452.

Wenders, Wim (1987) *Wings of desire.* Road Movies Filmproduktion/ Argos Films/ Westdeutscher Rundfunk.

Wilson, David Sloan (2021) 'How I come to bury Ayn Rand', *Nautilus,* 24/03/2021, retrieved on 6/04/2021 from https://nautil.us/issue/98/mind/i-have-come-to-bury-ayn-rand?utm_source=RSS_Feed&utm_medium=RSS&utm_campaign=RSS_Syndication&fbclid=IwAR0tyODHUzrSg_h9AZVQ6GmukuymxRbiTKV7cDE0rs0S2CKMaJ6nRHUP-dPk

Yeats, William Butler (1921) 'The second coming', *Michael Robartes and the dancer,* retrieved from http://www.theotherpages.org/poems/yeats02.html

Zueva, Anna (2021) 'Autoethnography through the folk tale lens', in: Monika Kostera and Nancy Harding (eds.) *Organizational ethnography.* Cheltenham: Edward Elgar, pp. 151-165.

Endnotes

1 If you have not heard of him, make sure to first look him up on the internet and watch one or two of his films, including *Coffee and Cigarettes,* 2003.

2 https://www.youtube.com/watch?v=KaOC9danxNo

3 https://polona.pl/item/reka-pracujaca-120-tablic-fotograficz nych,Mjg5ODM0NTE/100/#info:metadata

4 The translation misses the alliteration of the original: in Swedish all these words start with a 'b', an interesting poetic consonant as it produces an explosive sound, an entrance.

5 http://bunkier.art.pl/wp-content/uploads/2019/12/Piotr-Luty%C5%84ski_009.jpg

zer0
books

CULTURE, SOCIETY & POLITICS

Contemporary culture has eliminated the concept and public
figure of the intellectual. A cretinous anti-intellectualism
presides, cheer-led by hacks in the pay of multinational
corporations who reassure their bored readers that there is no
need to rouse themselves from their stupor. Zer0 Books knows
that another kind of discourse - intellectual without being
academic, popular without being populist - is not only possible:
it is already flourishing. Zer0 is convinced that in the unthinking,
blandly consensual culture in which we live, critical and engaged
theoretical reflection is more important than ever before.

If you have enjoyed this book, why not tell other readers by
posting a review on your preferred book site.

You may also wish to
subscribe to our Zer0 Books YouTube Channel.

Capitalist Realism
Is There No Alternative?
Mark Fisher
An analysis of the ways in which capitalism has presented itself
as the only realistic political-economic system.
Paperback: 978-1-84694-317-1 ebook: 978-1-78099-734-6

Rebel Rebel
Chris O'Leary
David Bowie: every single song. Everything you want to know,
everything you didn't know.
Paperback: 978-1-78099-244-0 ebook: 978-1-78099-713-1

Kill All Normies
Angela Nagle
Online culture wars from 4chan and Tumblr to Trump.
Paperback: 978-1-78535-543-1 ebook: 978-1-78535-544-8

Cartographies of the Absolute
Alberto Toscano, Jeff Kinkle
An aesthetics of the economy for the twenty-first century.
Paperback: 978-1-78099-275-4 ebook: 978-1-78279-973-3

Malign Velocities
Accelerationism and Capitalism
Benjamin Noys
Long listed for the Bread and Roses Prize 2015, *Malign Velocities*
argues against the need for speed, tracking acceleration as the
symptom of the ongoing crises of capitalism.
Paperback: 978-1-78279-300-7 ebook: 978-1-78279-299-4

Meat Market
Female Flesh under Capitalism
Laurie Penny
A feminist dissection of women's bodies as the fleshy fulcrum of
capitalist cannibalism, whereby women are both consumers and
consumed.
Paperback: 978-1-84694-521-2 ebook: 978-1-84694-782-7

Babbling Corpse
Vaporwave and the Commodification of Ghosts
Grafton Tanner
Paperback: 978-1-78279-759-3 ebook: 978-1-78279-760-9

New Work New Culture
Work we want and a culture that strengthens us
Frithjof Bergmann
A serious alternative for mankind and the planet.
Paperback: 978-1-78904-064-7 ebook: 978-1-78904-065-4

Romeo and Juliet in Palestine
Teaching Under Occupation
Tom Sperlinger
Life in the West Bank, the nature of pedagogy and the role of a
university under occupation.
Paperback: 978-1-78279-637-4 ebook: 978-1-78279-636-7

Color, Facture, Art and Design
Iona Singh
This materialist definition of fine-art develops guidelines for
architecture, design, cultural-studies and ultimately social
change.
Paperback: 978-1-78099-629-5 ebook: 978-1-78099-630-1

Sweetening the Pill
or How We Got Hooked on Hormonal Birth Control Holly Grigg-
Spall
Has contraception liberated or oppressed women?
Sweetening the Pill breaks the silence on the dark side of hormonal
contraception.
Paperback: 978-1-78099-607-3 ebook: 978-1-78099-608-0

Why Are We The Good Guys?
Reclaiming Your Mind from the Delusions of Propaganda
David Cromwell
A provocative challenge to the standard ideology that Western
power is a benevolent force in the world.
Paperback: 978-1-78099-365-2 ebook: 978-1-78099-366-9

The Writing on the Wall
On the Decomposition of Capitalism and its Critics Anselm
Jappe, Alastair Hemmens
A new approach to the meaning of social emancipation.
Paperback: 978-1-78535-581-3 ebook: 978-1-78535-582-0

Enjoying It
Candy Crush and Capitalism
Alfie Bown
A study of enjoyment and of the enjoyment of studying. Bown
asks what enjoyment says about us and what we say about
enjoyment, and why.
Paperback: 978-1-78535-155-6 ebook: 978-1-78535-156-3

Ghosts of My Life
Writings on Depression, Hauntology and Lost Futures
Mark Fisher
Paperback: 978-1-78099-226-6 ebook: 978-1-78279-624-4

Neglected or Misunderstood
The Radical Feminism of Shulamith Firestone
Victoria Margree
An interrogation of issues surrounding gender, biology,
sexuality, work and technology, and the ways in which our
imaginations continue to be in thrall to ideologies of maternity
and the nuclear family.
Paperback: 978-1-78535-539-4 ebook: 978-1-78535-540-0

How to Dismantle the NHS in 10 Easy Steps (Second Edition)
Youssef El-Gingihy
The story of how your NHS was sold off and why you will have
to buy private health insurance soon. A new expanded second
edition with chapters on junior doctors' strikes and government
blueprints for US-style healthcare.
Paperback: 978-1-78904-178-1 ebook: 978-1-78904-179-8

Digesting Recipes
The Art of Culinary Notation
Susannah Worth
A recipe is an instruction, the imperative tone of the expert, but
this constraint can offer its own kind of potential. A recipe need
not be a domestic trap but might instead offer escape – something
to fantasise about or aspire to.
Paperback: 978-1-78279-860-6 ebook: 978-1-78279-859-0

Most titles are published in paperback and as an ebook.
Paperbacks are available in traditional bookshops. Both print and
ebook formats are available online.
Follow us at:
https://www.facebook.com/ZeroBooks
https://twitter.com/Zer0Books
https://www.instagram.com/zero.Books